THE GOSPEL ACCORDING TO

MATTHEW

with Introduction by

Henry Wansbrough OSB

*All booklets are published thanks to the
generous support of the members of the
Catholic Truth Society*

CATHOLIC TRUTH SOCIETY
PUBLISHERS TO THE HOLY SEE

CONTENTS

The Jerusalem Bible translation

The Jerusalem Bible was first published in 1966. It was produced by a team of distinguished English scholars (including J.R.R. Tolkien), working under Alexander Jones. It made available for English readers the findings of the French *Bible de Jérusalem* published a decade earlier by the famous French biblical school in Jerusalem, the first Catholic Bible edition to incorporate all the advances of modern biblical study. The Jerusalem Bible was the first translation of the whole Bible into modern English, and as such has maintained its status as authorised for use in the liturgy.

❧ Introduction ❧

The Second Gospel comes First

Augustine of Hippo seems to have been responsible for putting the gospel of Matthew first in the order of the four gospels, and it is always printed at the head of the gospels. In the early Church it seems to have been the most popular and widespread of the gospels, and until the recent reforms of the Lectionary it was the gospel read most frequently in the liturgy. However, it was almost certainly the second gospel to be written, for it uses and expands on Mark, expressing Matthew's own particular angle on the Good News of Jesus. It contains far more of the teaching of Jesus than does Mark. Most scholars think that Matthew and Luke both drew this teaching from a collection of 'Sayings of the Lord' which has since disappeared, though some attribute the elaboration to Matthew's own work.

Matthew and Judaism

Matthew is the most Jewish of the gospels, insisting on every page that Jesus fulfils the promises of the Old Law. Jesus is a second David, adopted by Joseph into the House of David (1:20-25), addressed frequently as 'son of David' (1:1; 9:27; 15:22), and hailed as the messianic king of David's line (21:9). Matthew also depicts him as a second Moses (2:20, compare Exodus 3:19), who forms a new People of God, just as Moses formed the People of God in

3

the Old Testament (16:18). In Mark Jesus re-interpreted the Law; in Matthew Jesus gives a whole new Law, in the Sermon on the Mount, which perfects the old (5:17-20), bringing it to completion by interpreting it in accordance with the scriptural principle, 'What I want is love not sacrifice' (Hosea 6:6; Mt 9:13; 12:7; 23:23). So it is the old Law read in a new way. Nevertheless, Matthew is deeply Jewish in his thinking. He is much less absolute than Mark on the abolition of such Jewish practices as the Sabbath and the prohibitions of eating certain foods (compare Mk 7:20 with Mt 15:17). He shows Jesus acting always carefully in accordance with scriptural precedent (12:5, 11). With very rare exceptions, with habitual Jewish reverence he avoids using the name 'God', speaking of 'the Kingdom of Heaven' rather than 'the Kingdom of God'.

Yet at the same time there is stern criticism of current Judaism, Judaism as it was lived in Matthew's own day. The Jewish leaders, the scribes and Pharisees are heavily criticised for their concept of righteousness (5:20), for their hypocrisy (23:1-36), for their performance in public of the three classic good works of Judaism, fasting, prayer and almsgiving (6:1-18). Right at the beginning the Jewish King Herod is sharply contrasted with the gentile Magi, when he attempts to kill Jesus and they bring their gifts to the newborn child (2:1-16). Of the centurion of Capernaum Jesus says, 'nowhere in Israel have I found faith like this' (8:10). In his parables Matthew's gospel underlines that the

Jews are no longer the custodians of the Vineyard of Israel (21:43), and that their city is doomed to be destroyed (22:7). A hint of why this may be is occasionally given: 'they will flog you in their synagogues' (10:17) suggests a background of persecution of Christians by Jews - or rather, in Matthew's situation, of Christian Jews by Jews who did not accept Jesus as the Christ (11:21-24). They had failed to accept that something greater than Solomon (12:42), something greater than the Temple was present (12:6). Such a background of persecution and mutual hostility goes far to account for the terrible saying which has been at the root of so much Christian anti-Semitism, 'his blood be upon us and upon our children' (27:25).

The Exalted Christ

More clearly than in Mark, Jesus is an exalted figure, somehow as though he were already the Risen Christ. In some of the miracle-stories the crowd-scenes have melted away to leave a solemn and solitary confrontation between Jesus and the sufferer (compare Mk 1:29-31 with Mt 8:14-15, Mk 5:27 with Mt 9:20). His exalted status cannot remain hidden. At the final judgement it will be Jesus enthroned with his holy angels who exercises the divine prerogative of judgement (25:31). Far sooner than in Mark, human beings recognise Jesus as 'son of God', Peter confessing him as such when in Mark the disciples are still utterly puzzled (16:16; 14:33, compare Mk 6:51-

52). As Mark is the story of the gradual understanding of the meaning of Jesus as 'son of God', so Matthew goes one step further and is the revelation of what it means that through Jesus, God is with us. At the outset the child is to be named 'Emmanuel', which means 'God-with-us' (1:23), and at the end the Risen Christ promises to be always with his people (28:20, bracketing the gospel at beginning and end). In the great chapter on the community he promises that when two or three are gathered together, there he is in the midst of them (18:19). This promise is the source of their authority, which makes the decisions of the community binding also in heaven. Just as in the Old Testament the People of God is made holy by the presence of God among them, at first in the Tent of Meeting and later in the Temple, so the new People of God is made holy by the presence of Christ.

Matthew on the Community

While in Mark all the emphasis is on the arrival in Jesus of the Sovereignty or Kingdom of God, Matthew makes far more provision for the permanence of this community of the Church. In Mark Jesus makes little or no provision for the future of his community, as though the world might come to an end at any moment. In Matthew the promise of Christ's divine presence in the Church brings with it provision for a structure of authority, a machinery for achieving reconciliation (18:15-17), an authority for making decisions, conferred both on the community and on Peter himself (16:18; 18:18). Jesus' chosen Twelve will have a position of judgement, sitting on twelve thrones (19:28), though this does not contradict that all are still brothers in the Church (23:8-12). This may be the reason why Matthew quietly omits much of the criticism of the Twelve which occurs in Mark. There is a whole chapter on how missioners should behave and how they should be received (10:1-33). The need for continuing good works is emphasised: good works are like a wedding garment (22:11), like oil prepared for long-burning lamps (24:7), and will finally be the criterion on which all people will be judged (25:45).

Matthew's Poetry

Much of Matthew's power comes from what can only be described as his poetry. The rhythm of the sayings is beautifully balanced, often with a neat double opposition ('grapes from thorns or figs from thistles', 7:16; 'the harvest is rich but the labourers are few', 9:37). The same balance is seen in the parables. While Mark's parables are all about nature (seed, growth, harvest), all the long parables in Matthew are about people, contrasting good and bad in a black-and-white opposition: building a house on rock or sand (7:24-27), the ten wedding attendants (25:1-13), the sheep and the goats 25:31-46).

Matthew is a skilled teacher. He likes to use memorable and repeated formulas, 'You have learnt how it was

7

said..., but I say to you...' (5:21-48), or the formula 'this was to fulfil the prophecy'(8:17) with which he 14 times introduces an Old Testament quotation. The teaching of Jesus is easier to assimilate because it is gathered together into five great discourses arranged symmetrically: entry into the Kingdom (chapters 5-7, the Sermon on the Mount), external relations (10, the Mission Discourse), parables of the Kingdom (13), internal relations (18), final judgement in the Kingdom (24-25). His imagery helps to make the sayings memorable, for example the use of animals as symbols of qualities (cunning as serpents, harmless as doves, 10:16), and he delights in pairs of images, often contrasting (broad road and narrow gate, 7:13-14, bird's nest and foxhole, 8:20).

The Author

Who, then, was the author of this gospel? All the gospels were originally anonymous but this, 'according to Matthew', from the second century has been associated with the apostle Matthew, one of the Twelve. It is true that the name 'Matthew' is substituted for 'Levi' in Mark's story of the call of the apostle (Mk 2:14, Mt 9:9), but it is hard to believe that anyone would recount his own call by Jesus in the words of another. This apostle would also have been of a great age when it came to the detailed work of composing this finely-honed work, for it must have been written well after Mark (65-75 AD).

Perhaps Matthew sponsored the gospel as the authentic message of Christ; perhaps it is merely the gospel in which the story about Matthew occurs. The question must remain open; the name of the author is not of paramount importance. At least the attitude to Judaism fits the relationship of Judaism and Christianity right at the end of the first century. It has been suggested that the place of composition was Antioch on the Syrian coast, a great city which contained an important Jewish colony, a significant number of whom became Christians. It is the only gospel quoted by Ignatius, Bishop of Antioch in his letters written about 108AD.

Reading Matthew

In reading Matthew it might be useful to be alert especially to the way Matthew, though describing Jesus' life on earth, is clearly aware that he is now the Risen Lord. Matthew is strongly conscious that Christ is present in his community - without his presence the ship of the Church is lost - and of Christ's work carried out by the members of the community.

THE GOSPEL ACCORDING TO
☙ MATTHEW ❧

I. THE BIRTH AND INFANCY OF JESUS

The ancestry of Jesus

1 ¹A genealogy of Jesus Christ, son of David, son of Abraham:[a]

²Abraham was the father of Isaac,

Isaac the father of Jacob,

Jacob the father of Judah and his brothers,

³Judah was the father of Perez and Zerah,

    Tamar being their mother,

Perez was the father of Hezron,

Hezron the father of Ram,

⁴Ram was the father of Amminadab,

Amminadab the father of Nahshon,

Nahshon the father of Salmon,

⁵Salmon was the father of Boaz,

    Rahab being his mother,

Boaz was the father of Obed, Ruth being his mother,

Obed was the father of Jesse;

⁶and Jesse was the father of King David.

David was the father of Solomon,

[a.] Showing the descent of Joseph, legally the father of Jesus, from Abraham and David, to whom the messianic promises were made.

whose mother had been Uriah's wife,
[7]Solomon was the father of Rehoboam,
Rehoboam the father of Abijah,
Abijah the father of Asa,
[8]Asa was the father of Jehoshaphat,
Jehoshaphat the father of Joram,
Joram the father of Azariah,
[9]Azariah was the father of Jotham,
Jotham the father of Ahaz,
Ahaz the father of Hezekiah,
[10]Hezekiah was the father of Manasseh,
Manasseh the father of Amon,
Amon the father of Josiah;
[11]and Josiah was the father of Jechoniah and his brothers.
Then the deportation to Babylon took place.

[12]After the deportation to Babylon:
Jechoniah was the father of Shealtiel,
Shealtiel the father of Zerubbabel,
[13]Zerubbabel was the father of Abiud,
Abiud the father of Eliakim,
Eliakim the father of Azor,
[14]Azor was the father of Zadok,
Zadok the father of Achim,
Achim the father of Eliud,
[15]Eliud was the father of Eleazar,
Eleazar the father of Matthan,

Matthan the father of Jacob;
¹⁶and Jacob was the father of Joseph the husband of Mary;
of her was born Jesus who is called Christ.
¹⁷The sum of generations is therefore: fourteen from Abraham to David; fourteen from David to the Babylonian deportation; and fourteen from the Babylonian deportation to Christ.

The virginal conception of Christ

¹⁸This is how Jesus Christ came to be born. His mother Mary was betrothed to Joseph;[b] but before they came to live together she was found to be with child through the Holy Spirit. ¹⁹Her husband Joseph; being a man of honour and wanting to spare her publicity, decided to divorce her informally. ²⁰He had made up his mind to do this when the angel of the Lord appeared to him in a dream and said, 'Joseph son of David, do not be afraid to take Mary home as your wife, because she has conceived what is in her by the Holy Spirit. ²¹She will give birth to a son and you must name him Jesus, because he is the one who is to save[c] his people from their sins.' ²²Now all this took place to fulfil the words spoken by the Lord through the prophet:

> ²³ *'The virgin will conceive and give birth to a son*
> *and they will call him Emmanuel,*[d]

[1 b.] In a Jewish betrothal the man was already called the 'husband' of the woman, and he could release himself from the engagement only by an act of repudiation, v.19.

[1 c.] 'Jesus' (Hebr. Yehoshua) means 'Yahweh saves'.

[1 d.] Is 7:14

a name which means 'God-is-with-us'. ²⁴When Joseph woke up he did what the angel of the Lord had told him to do: he took his wife to his home ²⁵and, though he had not had intercourse with her, she gave birth to a son; and he named him Jesus.

The visit of the Magi

2 ¹After Jesus had been born at Bethlehem in Judaea during the reign of King Herod,ª some wise men came to Jerusalem from the east. ²'Where is the infant king of the Jews?' they asked. 'We saw his star as it roseᵇ and have come to do him homage.' ³When King Herod heard this he was perturbed, and so was the whole of Jerusalem. ⁴He called together all the chief priests and the scribes of the people, and enquired of them where the Christ was to be born. ⁵'At Bethlehem in Judaea,' they told him 'for this is what the prophet wrote:

⁶And you, Bethlehem, in the land of Judah,
you are by no means least among the leaders of Judah,
for out of you will come a leader
who will shepherd my people Israel'.ᶜ

⁷Then Herod summoned the wise men to see him privately. He asked them the exact date on which the star had appeared, ⁸and sent them on to Bethlehem. 'Go and

---

²ᵃ· About 5 or 4 B.C. Herod was king of Judaea, Idumaea and Samaria from 37-4 B.C.
²ᵇ· 'In the east' is an alternative translation, here and in v.9.
²ᶜ· Mi 5:1

find out all about the child,' he said 'and when you have found him, let me know, so that I too may go and do him homage.' [9]Having listened to what the king had to say, they set out. And there in front of them was the star they had seen rising; it went forward, and halted over the place where the child was. [10]The sight of the star filled them with delight, [11]and going into the house they saw the child with his mother Mary, and falling to their knees they did him homage. Then, opening their treasures, they offered him gifts of gold and frankincense and myrrh.[d] [12]But they were warned in a dream not to go back to Herod, and returned to their own country by a different way.

The flight into Egypt. The massacre of the Innocents

[13]After they had left, the angel of the Lord appeared to Joseph in a dream and said, 'Get up, take the child and his mother with you, and escape into Egypt, and stay there until I tell you, because Herod intends to search for the child and do away with him'. [14]So Joseph got up and, taking the child and his mother with him, left that night for Egypt, [15]where he stayed until Herod was dead. This was to fulfil what the Lord had spoken through the prophet:

I called my son out of Egypt.[e]

[16]Herod was furious when he realised that he had been outwitted by the wise men, and in Bethlehem and its

---

[2 d.] The wealth and perfumes of Arabia.
[2 e.] Ho 11:1

surrounding district he had all the male children killed who were two years old or under, reckoning by the date he had been careful to ask the wise men. [17]It was then that the words spoken through the prophet Jeremiah were fulfilled:

[18]A voice was heard in Ramah,
sobbing and loudly lamenting:
it was Rachel weeping for her children,
refusing to be comforted
because they were no more.[f]

From Egypt to Nazareth

[19]After Herod's death, the angel of the Lord appeared in a dream to Joseph in Egypt [20]and said, 'Get up, take the child and his mother with you and go back to the land of Israel, for those who wanted to kill the child are dead'. [21]So Joseph got up and, taking the child and his mother with him, went back to the land of Israel. [22]But when he learnt that Archelaus[g] had succeeded his father Herod as ruler of Judaea he was afraid to go there, and being warned in a dream he left for the region of Galilee.[h] [23]There he settled in a town called Nazareth. In this way the words spoken through the prophets were to be fulfilled:

'He will be called a Nazarene.'

---

2 f. Jr 31: 15
2 g. Ethnarch of Judaea, 4 B.C. to A.D. 6.
2 h. The territory of Herod Antipas.

II. The Kingdom of Heaven Proclaimed

A. Narrative Section

The preaching of John the Baptist

3 [1]In due course John the Baptist appeared; he preached in the wilderness of Judaea and this was his message: [2]'Repent, for the kingdom of heaven[a] is close at hand'. [3]This was the man the prophet Isaiah spoke of when he said:

A voice cries in the wilderness:
Prepare a way for the Lord,
make his paths straight.[b]

[4]This man John wore a garment made of camel-hair with a leather belt round his waist, and his food was locusts and wild honey. [5]Then Jerusalem and all Judaea and the whole Jordan district made their way to him, [6]and as they were baptised by him in the river Jordan they confessed their sins. [7]But when he saw a number of Pharisees and Sadducees[c] coming for baptism he said to them, [8]'Brood of vipers, who warned you to fly from the retribution that is coming? But if you are repentant, produce the appropriate fruit, [9]and do not presume to tell yourselves, "We have Abraham for our father", because, I tell you, God can raise

---

[3a.] 'kingdom of God'; Mt's phrase reflects the Jewish scruple against using the name of God.
[3b.] Is 40:3
[3c.] Pharisees: members of a Jewish sect known for its strict observance of the Law as it was interpreted and developed by their rabbis. Sadducees: conservatives who observed the written form of the Law in the scriptures.

children for Abraham from these stones. ¹⁰Even now the axe is laid to the roots of the trees, so that any tree which fails to produce good fruit will be cut down and thrown on the fire. ¹¹I baptise you in water for repentance, but the one who follows me is more powerful than I am, and I am not fit to carry his sandals; he will baptise you with the Holy Spirit and fire. ¹²His winnowing-fan is in his hand; he will clear his threshing-floor and gather his wheat into the barn; but the chaff he will burn in a fire that will never go out.'

Jesus is baptised

¹³Then Jesus appeared: he came from Galilee to the Jordan to be baptised by John. ¹⁴John tried to dissuade him. 'It is I who need baptism from you' he said 'and yet you come to me!' ¹⁵But Jesus replied, 'Leave it like this for the time being; it is fitting that we should, in this way, do all that righteousness demands'. At this, John gave in to him.

¹⁶As soon as Jesus was baptised he came up from the water, and suddenly the heavens opened and he saw the Spirit of God descending like a dove and coming down on him. ¹⁷And a voice spoke from heaven, 'This is my Son, the Beloved; my favour rests on him'.

Temptation in the wilderness

4 ¹Then Jesus was led by the Spirit out into the wilderness to be tempted by the devil. ²He fasted for forty days and forty nights, after which he was very hungry, ³and the tempter came and said to him, 'If you

are the Son of God, tell these stones to turn into loaves'.
⁴But he replied, 'Scripture says:

Man does not live on bread alone
but on every word that comes from the mouth of God'.[a]

⁵The devil then took him to the holy city and made him stand on the parapet of the Temple. ⁶'If you are the Son of God' he said 'throw yourself down; for scripture says:

He will put you in his angels' charge,
and they will support you on their hands
in case you hurt your foot against a stone'.[b]

⁷Jesus said to him, 'Scripture also says:

You must not put the Lord your God to the test'.[c]

⁸Next, taking him to a very high mountain, the devil showed him all the kingdoms of the world and their splendour. ⁹'I will give you all these' he said, 'if you fall at my feet and worship me.' ¹⁰Then Jesus replied, 'Be off, Satan! For scripture says:

You must worship the Lord your God,
and serve him alone.'[d]

¹¹Then the devil left him, and angels appeared and looked after him.

Return to Galilee

¹²Hearing that John had been arrested he went back to Galilee, ¹³and leaving Nazareth he went and settled in Capernaum, a

---

[a] Dt 8:3
[b] Ps 91:11-12
[c] Dt 6:16
[d] Dt 6:13

lakeside town on the borders of Zebulun and Naphtali. [14]In this way the prophecy of Isaiah was to be fulfilled:

> [15]*'Land of Zebulun! Land of Naphtali!*
> *Way of the sea on the far side of Jordan,*
> *Galilee of the nations!*
> [16]*The people that lived in darkness*
> *has seen a great light;*
> *on those who dwell in the land and shadow of death*
> *a light has dawned.'*[e]

[17]From that moment Jesus began his preaching with the message, 'Repent, for the kingdom of heaven is close at hand'.

The first four disciples are called

[18]As he was walking by the Sea of Galilee he saw two brothers, Simon, who was called Peter, and his brother Andrew; they were making a cast in the lake with their net, for they were fishermen. [19]And he said to them, 'Follow me and I will make you fishers of men'. [20]And they left their nets at once and followed him.

[21]Going on from there he saw another pair of brothers, James son of Zebedee and his brother John; they were in their boat with their father Zebedee, mending their nets, and he called them. [22]At once, leaving the boat and their father, they followed him.

Jesus preaches and heals the sick

[23]He went round the whole of Galilee teaching in their

---

[e]. Is 8:23-9:1

synagogues, proclaiming the Good News of the kingdom and curing all kinds of diseases and sickness among the people. [24]His fame spread throughout Syria,[f] and those who were suffering from diseases and painful complaints of one kind or another, the possessed, epileptics, the paralysed, were all brought to him, and he cured them. [25]Large crowds followed him, coming from Galilee, the Decapolis,[g] Jerusalem, Judaea and Transjordania.

B. The Sermon on the Mount[a]

The Beatitudes

5 [1]Seeing the crowds, he went up the hill. There he sat down and was joined by his disciples. [2]Then he began to speak. This is what he taught them:

[3]'How happy are the poor in spirit;
theirs is the kingdom of heaven.

[4]Happy *the gentle:*[b]
they shall have the earth for their heritage.

[5]Happy those who mourn:
they shall be comforted.

[6]Happy those who hunger and thirst for what is right:
they shall be satisfied.

[4f.] i.e. Galilee and the districts listed in v.25.

[4g.] The 'ten towns', a region south-east of Galilee.

[5a.] In this discourse, which occupies three ch. of this gospel, Mt has included sayings which probably originated on other occasions (cf. their parallels in Lk).

[5b.] Or 'the lowly'; the word comes from the Greek version of Ps 37.

⁷Happy the merciful:
they shall have mercy shown them.
⁸Happy the pure in heart:
they shall see God.
⁹Happy the peacemakers:
they shall be called sons of God.
¹⁰Happy those who are persecuted in the cause of right:
theirs is the kingdom of heaven.
¹¹'Happy are you when people abuse you and persecute you and speak all kinds of calumny against you on my account. ¹²Rejoice and be glad, for your reward will be great in heaven; this is how they persecuted the prophets before you.

Salt of the earth and light of the world

¹³'You are the salt of the earth. But if salt becomes tasteless, what can make it salty again? It is good for nothing, and can only be thrown out to be trampled underfoot by men.

¹⁴'You are the light of the world. A city built on a hilltop cannot be hidden. ¹⁵No one lights a lamp to put it under a tub; they put it on the lamp-stand where it shines for everyone in the house. ¹⁶In the same way your light must shine in the sight of men, so that, seeing your good works, they may give the praise to your Father in heaven.

The fulfilment of the Law

¹⁷'Do not imagine that I have come to abolish the Law or the Prophets. I have come not to abolish but to complete

them. [18]I tell you solemnly, till heaven and earth disappear, not one dot, not one little stroke, shall disappear from the Law until its purpose is achieved. [19]Therefore, the man who infringes even one of the least of these commandments and teaches others to do the same will be considered the least in the kingdom of heaven; but the man who keeps them and teaches them will be considered great in the kingdom of heaven.

The new standard higher than the old

[20]'For I tell you, if your virtue goes no deeper than that of the scribes and Pharisees, you will never get into the kingdom of heaven.

[21]'You have learnt how it was said to our ancestors: *You must not kill;*[c] and if anyone does kill he must answer for it before the court. [22]But I say this to you: anyone who is angry with his brother will answer for it before the court; if a man calls his brother "Fool"[d] he will answer for it before the Sanhedrin;[e] and if a man calls him "Renegade"[f] he will answer for it in hell fire. [23]So then, if you are bringing your offering to the altar and there remember that your brother has something against you, [24]leave your offering there before the altar, go and be reconciled with your brother first, and then come back and present your offering. [25]Come

---

5 c. Ex 20:13
5 d. Translating an Aramaic term of contempt.
5 e. The High Court at Jerusalem.
5 f. Apostasy was the most repulsive of all sins.

to terms with your opponent in good time while you are still on the way to the court with him, or he may hand you over to the judge and the judge to the officer, and you will be thrown into prison. [26]I tell you solemnly, you will not get out till you have paid the last penny.

[27]'You have learnt how it was said: *You must not commit adultery*[g]. [28]But I say this to you: if a man looks at a woman lustfully, he has already committed adultery with her in his heart. [29]If your right eye should cause you to sin, tear it out and throw it away; for it will do you less harm to lose one part of you than to have your whole body thrown into hell. [30]And if your right hand should cause you to sin, cut it off and throw it away; for it will do you less harm to lose one part of you than to have your whole body go to hell.

[31]'It has also been said: *Anyone who divorces his wife must give her a writ of dismissal.*[h] [32]But I say this to you: everyone who divorces his wife, except for the case of fornication, makes her an adulteress; and anyone who marries a divorced woman commits adultery.

[33]'Again, you have learnt how it was said to our ancestors: *You must not break your oath, but must fulfil your oaths to the Lord.*[i] [34]But I say this to you: do not swear at all, either by *heaven*, since that is God's throne; [35]or by *the earth*, since that is *his footstool*; or by

---

[5g.] Ex 20:14
[5h.] Dt 24:1
[5i.] Ex 20:7

Jerusalem, since that is *the city of the great king.* [36]Do not swear by your own head either, since you cannot turn a single hair white or black. [37]All you need say is "Yes" if you mean yes, "No" if you mean no; anything more than this comes from the evil one.

[38]'You have learnt how it was said: *Eye for eye and tooth for tooth.*[j] [39]But I say this to you: offer the wicked man no resistance. On the contrary, if anyone hits you on the right cheek, offer him the other as well; [40]if a man takes you to law and would have your tunic, let him have your cloak as well. [41]And if anyone orders you to go one mile, go two miles with him. [42]Give to anyone who asks, and if anyone wants to borrow, do not turn away.

[43]'You have learnt how it was said: *You must love your neighbour and hate your enemy.*[k] [44]But I say this to you: love your enemies and pray for those who persecute you; [45]in this way you will be sons of your Father in heaven, for he causes his sun to rise on bad men as well as good, and his rain to fall on honest and dishonest men alike. [46]For if you love those who love you, what right have you to claim any credit? Even the tax collectors[l] do as much, do they not? [47]And if you save your greetings for your

---

[5j.] Ex 21:24

[5k.] The quotation is from Lv 19:18; the second part of this commandment, not in the written Law, is an Aramaic way of saying 'You do not have to love your enemy'.

[5l.] They were employed by the occupying power and this earned them popular contempt.

brothers, are you doing anything exceptional? Even the pagans do as much, do they not? [48]You must therefore be perfect just as your heavenly Father is perfect.

Almsgiving in secret

6 [1]'Be careful not to parade your good deeds before men to attract their notice; by doing this you will lose all reward from your Father in heaven. [2]So when you give alms, do not have it trumpeted before you; this is what the hypocrites do in the synagogues and in the streets to win men's admiration. I tell you solemnly, they have had their reward. [3]But when you give alms, your left hand must not know what your right is doing; [4]your almsgiving must be secret, and your Father who sees all that is done in secret will reward you.

Prayer in secret

[5]'And when you pray, do not imitate the hypocrites: they love to say their prayers standing up in the synagogues and at the street corners for people to see them; I tell you solemnly, they have had their reward. [6]But when you pray, *go to your private room and, when you have shut your door, pray*[a] to your Father who is in that secret place, and your Father who sees all that is done in secret will reward you.

How to pray. The Lord's Prayer

[7]'In your prayers do not babble as the pagans do, for they

[6 a.] Not a direct quotation but an allusion to the practice common in the O.T., see 2 K 4:33.

26

think that by using many words they will make themselves heard. [8]Do not be like them; your Father knows what you need before you ask him. [9]So you should pray like this:

'Our Father in heaven,
may your name be held holy,
[10]your kingdom come,
your will be done,
on earth as in heaven.
[11]Give us today our daily bread.
[12]And forgive us our debts,
as we have forgiven those who are in debt to us.
[13]And do not put us to the test,
but save us from the evil one.

[14]'Yes, if you forgive others their failings, your heavenly Father will forgive you yours; [15]but if you do not forgive others, your Father will not forgive your failings either.

Fasting in secret

[16]'When you fast do not put on a gloomy look as the hypocrites do: they pull long faces to let men know they are fasting. I tell you solemnly, they have had their reward. [17]But when you fast, put oil on your head and wash your face, [18]so that no one will know you are fasting except your Father who sees all that is done in secret; and your Father who sees all that is done in secret will reward you.

True treasures

[19]'Do not store up treasures for yourselves on earth, where

moths and woodworms destroy them and thieves can break in and steal. [20]But store up treasures for yourselves in heaven, where neither moth nor woodworms destroy them and thieves cannot break in and steal. [21]For where your treasure is, there will your heart be also.

The eye, the lamp of the body

[22]'The lamp of the body is the eye. It follows that if your eye is sound, your whole body will be filled with light. [23]But if your eye is diseased, your whole body will be all darkness. If then, the light inside you is darkness, what darkness that will be!

God and money

[24]"No one can be the slave of two masters: he will either hate the first and love the second, or treat the first with respect and the second with scorn. You cannot be the slave both of God and of money.

Trust in Providence

[25]'That is why I am telling you not to worry about your life and what you are to eat, nor about your body and how you are to clothe it. Surely life means more than food, and the body more than clothing! [26]Look at the birds in the sky. They do not sow or reap or gather into barns; yet your heavenly Father feeds them. Are we not worth much more than they are? [27]Can any of you, for all his worrying, add one single cubit to his span of life?

²⁸And why worry about clothing? Think of the flowers growing in the fields; they never have to work or spin; ²⁹yet I assure you that not even Solomon in all his regalia was robed like one of these. ³⁰Now if that is how God clothes the grass in the field which is there today and thrown into the furnace tomorrow, will he not much more look after you, you men of little faith? ³¹So do not worry; do not say, "What are we to eat? What are we to drink? How are we to be clothed?" ³²It is the pagans who set their hearts on all these things. Your heavenly Father knows you need them all. ³³Set your hearts on his kingdom first, and on his righteousness, and all these other things will be given you as well. ³⁴So do not worry about tomorrow: tomorrow will take care of itself. Each day has enough trouble of its own.

Do not judge

7 ¹"Do not judge, and you will not be judged; ²because the judgements you give are the judgements you will get, and the amount you measure out is the amount you will be given. ³Why do you observe the splinter in your brother's eye and never notice the plank in your own? ⁴How dare you say to your brother, "Let me take the splinter out of your eye", when all the time there is a plank in your own? ⁵Hypocrite! Take the plank out of your own eye first, and then you will see clearly enough to take the splinter out of your brother's eye.

Do not profane sacred things

[6]'Do not give dogs what is holy;[a] and do not throw your pearls in front of pigs, or they may trample them and then turn on you and tear you to pieces.

Effective prayer

[7]'Ask, and it will be given to you; search, and you will find; knock, and the door will be opened to you. [8]For the one who asks always receives; the one who searches always finds; the one who knocks will always have the door opened to him. [9]Is there a man among you who would hand his son a stone when he asked for bread? [10]Or would hand him a snake when he asked for a fish? [11]If you, then, who are evil, know how to give your children what is good, how much more will your Father in heaven give good things to those who ask him!

The golden rule

[12]'So always treat others as you would like them to treat you; that is the meaning of the Law and the Prophets.

The two ways

[13]'Enter by the narrow gate, since the road that leads to perdition is wide and spacious, and many take it; [14]but it is a narrow gate and a hard road that leads to life, and only a few find it.

[7a]. The meat of animals which have been offered in sacrifice in the Temple; the application is to the parading of holy beliefs and practices in front of those who cannot understand them.

False prophets

[15]'Beware of false prophets[b] who come to you disguised as sheep but underneath are ravenous wolves. [16]You will be able to tell them by their fruits. Can people pick grapes from thorns, or figs from thistles? [17]In the same way, a sound tree produces good fruit but a rotten tree bad fruit. [18]A sound tree cannot bear bad fruit, nor a rotten tree bear good fruit. [19]Any tree that does not produce good fruit is cut down and thrown on the fire. [20]I repeat, you will be able to tell them by their fruits.

The true disciple

[21]'It is not those who say to me, "Lord, Lord", who will enter the kingdom of heaven, but the person who does the will of my Father in heaven. [22]When the day[c] comes many will say to me, "Lord, Lord, did we not prophesy in your name, cast out demons in your name, work many miracles in your name?" [23]Then I shall tell them to their faces: I have never known you; *away from me, you evil men!'*

[24]'Therefore, everyone who listens to these words of mine and acts on them will be like a sensible man who built his house on rock. [25]Rain came down, floods rose, gales blew and hurled themselves against that house, and it did not fall: it was founded on rock. [26]But everyone who listens to these words of mine and does not act on them

---

[7 b.] Lying teachers of religion.
[7 c.] The day of Judgement.

will be like a stupid man who built his house on sand. [27]Rain came down, floods rose, gales blew and struck that house, and it fell; and what a fall it had!'

The amazement of the crowds

[28]Jesus had now finished what he wanted to say, and his teaching made a deep impression on the people [29]because he taught them with authority, and not like their own scribes.[d]

III. THE KINGDOM OF HEAVEN IS PREACHED

A. Narrative Section: Ten Miracles

Cure of a leper

8[1]After he had come down from the mountain large crowds followed him. [2]A leper now came up and bowed low in front of him. 'Sir,' he said 'if you want to, you can cure me.' [3]Jesus stretched out his hand, touched him and said, 'Of course I want to! Be cured!' And his leprosy was cured at once. [4]Then Jesus said to him, 'Mind you do not tell anyone, but go and show yourself to the priest and make the offering prescribed by Moses, as evidence for them'.

Cure of the centurion's servant

[5]When he went into Capernaum a centurion came up and pleaded with him. [6]'Sir,' he said 'my servant is lying at home paralysed, and in great pain.' [7]'I will come myself and cure him'

[7 d.] Doctors of the law, who buttressed their teaching by quotation from the scriptures and traditions.

said Jesus. [8]The centurion replied, 'Sir, I am not worthy to have you under my roof; just give the word and my servant will be cured. [9]For I am under authority myself, and have soldiers under me; and I say to one man: Go, and he goes; to another: Come here, and he comes; to my servant: Do this, and he does it.' [10]When Jesus heard this he was astonished and said to those following him, 'I tell you solemnly, nowhere in Israel have I found faith like this. [11]And I tell you that many will come from east and west to take their places with Abraham and Isaac and Jacob at the feast in the kingdom of heaven; [12]but the subjects of the kingdom[a] will be turned out into the dark, where there will be weeping and grinding of teeth.' [13]And to the centurion Jesus said, 'Go back, then; you have believed, so let this be done for you'. And the servant was cured at that moment.

Cure of Peter's mother-in-law

[14]And going into Peter's house Jesus found Peter's mother-in-law in bed with fever. [15]He touched her hand and the fever left her, and she got up and began to wait on him.

A number of cures

[16]That evening they brought him many who were possessed by devils. He cast out the spirits with a word and cured all who were sick. [17]This was to fulfil the prophecy of Isaiah:

> *He took our sicknesses away and carried*
> *our diseases for us.*[b]

[8a.] The Jews, natural heirs of the promises.
[8b.] Is 53:4

Hardships of the apostolic calling

[18]When Jesus saw the great crowds all about him he gave orders to leave for the other side.[c] [19]One of the scribes then came up and said to him, 'Master, I will follow you wherever you go'. [20]Jesus replied, 'Foxes have holes and the birds of the air have nests, but the Son of Man has nowhere to lay his head'.

[21]Another man, one of his disciples, said to him, 'Sir, let me go and bury my father first'. [22]But Jesus replied, 'Follow me, and leave the dead to bury their dead'.

The calming of the storm

[23]Then he got into the boat followed by his disciples. [24]Without warning a storm broke over the lake, so violent that the waves were breaking right over the boat. But he was asleep. [25]So they went to him and woke him saying, 'Save us, Lord, we are going down!' [26]And he said to them, 'Why are you so frightened, you men of little faith?' And with that he stood up and rebuked the winds and the sea; and all was calm again. [27]The men were astounded and said, 'Whatever kind of man is this? Even the winds and the sea obey him.'

The demoniacs of Gadara

[28]When he reached the country of the Gadarenes on the other side, two demoniacs came towards him out of the tombs - creatures so fierce that no one could pass that way.

---

8 c. The east bank of Lake Tiberias.

[29]They stood there shouting, 'What do you want with us, Son of God? Have you come here to torture us before the time?'[d] [30]Now some distance away there was a large herd of pigs feeding, [31]and the devils pleaded with Jesus, 'If you cast us out, send us into the herd of pigs'. [32]And he said to them, 'Go then', and they came out and made for the pigs; and at that the whole herd charged down the cliff into the lake and perished in the water. [33]The swineherds ran off and made for the town, where they told the whole story, including what had happened to the demoniacs. [34]At this the whole town set out to meet Jesus; and as soon as they saw him they implored him to leave the neighbourhood.

Cure of a paralytic

9 [1]He got back in the boat, crossed the water and came to his own town.[a] [2]Then some people appeared, bringing him a paralytic stretched out on a bed. Seeing their faith, Jesus said to the paralytic, 'Courage, my child, your sins are forgiven'. [3]And at this some scribes said to themselves, 'This man is blaspheming'. [4]Knowing what was in their minds Jesus said, 'Why do you have such wicked thoughts in your hearts? [5]Now, which of these is easier to say, "Your sins are forgiven", or to say, "Get up and walk"? [6]But to prove to you that the Son of Man has authority on earth to forgive sins,' - he said to the

[8 d.] The day of Judgement, when the reign of God would banish all demons.
[9 a.] Capernaum, cf. 4:13.

paralytic - 'get up, and pick up your bed and go off home'. [7]And the man got up and went home. [8]A feeling of awe came over the crowd when they saw this, and they praised God for giving such power to men.

The call of Matthew

[9]As Jesus was walking on from there he saw a man named Matthew[b] sitting by the customs house, and he said to him, 'Follow me'. And he got up and followed him.

Eating with sinners

[10]While he was at dinner in the house it happened that a number of tax collectors and sinners[c] came to sit at the table with Jesus and his disciples. [11]When the Pharisees saw this, they said to his disciples, 'Why does your master eat with tax collectors and sinners?' [12]When he heard this he replied, 'It is not the healthy who need the doctor, but the sick. [13]Go and learn the meaning of the words: *What I want is mercy, not sacrifice.*[d] And indeed I did not come to call the virtuous, but sinners.'

A discussion on fasting

[14]Then John's[e] disciples came to him and said, 'Why is it that we and the Pharisees fast, but your disciples do not?'

[9b.] Called Levi by Mk and Lk.
[9c.] Social outcasts, made 'unclean' by breaking religious laws or following a disreputable profession.
[9d.] Ho 6:6
[9e.] John the Baptist.

[15]Jesus replied, 'Surely the bridegroom's attendants would never think of mourning as long as the bridegroom is still with them? But the time will come for the bridegroom to be taken away from them, and then they will fast. [16]No one puts a piece of unshrunken cloth on to an old cloak, because the patch pulls away from the cloak and the tear gets worse. [17]Nor do people put new wine into old wineskins; if they do, the skins burst, the wine runs out, and the skins are lost. No; they put new wine into fresh skins and both are preserved.'[f]

Cure of the woman with a haemorrhage.
The official's daughter raised to life

[18]While he was speaking to them, up came one of the officials, who bowed low in front of him and said, 'My daughter has just died, but come and lay your hand on her and her life will be saved'. [19]Jesus rose and, with his disciples, followed him.

[20]Then from behind him came a woman, who had suffered from a haemorrhage for twelve years, and she touched the fringe of his cloak, [21]for she said to herself, 'If I can only touch his cloak I shall be well again'. [22]Jesus turned round and saw her; and he said to her, 'Courage, my daughter, your faith has restored you to health'. And from that moment the woman was well again.

---

[9] f. New devotional exercises, like those which John and the Pharisees add to the religion of the old order, will not preserve it.

²³When Jesus reached the official's house and saw the flute-players, with the crowd making a commotion^g he said, ²⁴'Get out of here; the little girl is not dead, she is asleep'. And they laughed at him. ²⁵But when the people had been turned out he went inside and took the little girl by the hand; and she stood up. ²⁶And the news spread all round the countryside.

Cure of two blind men

²⁷As Jesus went on his way two blind men followed him shouting, 'Take pity on us, Son of David'. ²⁸And when Jesus reached the house the blind men came up with him and he said to them, 'Do you believe I can do this?' They said, 'Sir, we do'. ²⁹Then he touched their eyes saying, 'Your faith deserves it, so let this be done for you'. ³⁰And their sight returned. Then Jesus sternly warned them, 'Take care that no one learns about this'. ³¹But when they had gone, they talked about him all over the countryside.

Cure of a dumb demoniac

³²They had only just left when a man was brought to him, a dumb demoniac. ³³And when the devil was cast out, the dumb man spoke and the people were amazed. 'Nothing like this has ever been seen in Israel' they said. ³⁴But the Pharisees said, 'It is through the prince of devils that he casts out devils'.

The distress of the crowds

³⁵Jesus made a tour through all the towns and villages,

---

⁹ ᵍ The loud wailing of the oriental mourner.

teaching in their synagogues, proclaiming the Good News of the kingdom and curing all kinds of diseases and sickness. 36And when he saw the crowds he felt sorry for them because they were harassed and dejected, like sheep without a shepherd. 37Then he said to his disciples, 'The harvest is rich but the labourers are few, so ask the Lord of the harvest to send labourers to his harvest'.

B. The Instruction of the Apostles

The mission of the Twelve

10 1He summoned his twelve disciples, and gave them authority over unclean spirits with power to cast them out and to cure all kinds of diseases and sickness.

2These are the names of the twelve apostles: first, Simon who is called Peter, and his brother Andrew; James the son of Zebedee, and his brother John; 3Philip and Bartholomew; Thomas, and Matthew the tax collector; James the son of Alphaeus, and Thaddaeus; 4Simon the Zealot and Judas Iscariot, the one who was to betray him. 5These twelve Jesus sent out, instructing them as follows:

'Do not turn your steps to pagan territory, and do not enter any Samaritan town; 6go rather to the lost sheep of the House of Israel. 7And as you go, proclaim that the kingdom of heaven is close at hand. 8Cure the sick, raise the dead, cleanse the lepers, cast out devils. You received without charge, give without charge. 9Provide yourselves with no gold or silver, not even with a few coppers for your purses,

[10]with no haversack for the journey or spare tunic or footwear or a staff, for the workman deserves his keep.

[11]'Whatever town or village you go into, ask for someone trustworthy and stay with him until you leave. [12]As you enter his house, salute it, [13]and if the house deserves it, let your peace descend upon it; if it does not, let your peace come back to you. [14]And if anyone does not welcome you or listen to what you have to say, as you walk out of the house or town shake the dust from your feet. [15]I tell you solemnly, on the day of Judgement it will not go as hard with the land of Sodom and Gomorrah as with that town. [16]Remember, I am sending you out like sheep among wolves; so be cunning as serpents and yet as harmless as doves.

The missionaries will be persecuted[a]

[17]'Beware of men: they will hand you over to sanhedrins and scourge you in their synagogues. [18]You will be dragged before governors and kings for my sake, to bear witness before them and the pagans. [19]But when they hand you over, do not worry about how to speak or what to say; what you are to say will be given to you when the time comes; [20]because it is not you who will be speaking; the Spirit of your Father will be speaking in you.

[21]'Brother will betray brother to death, and the father his child; children will rise against their parents and

---

[10]a. The conditions described in vv. 17-39 are those of a later time than this first mission of the Twelve.

have them put to death. [22]You will be hated by all men on account of my name; but the man who stands firm to the end will be saved. [23]If they persecute you in one town, take refuge in the next; and if they persecute you in that, take refuge in another. I tell you solemnly, you will not have gone the round of the towns of Israel before the Son of Man comes.

[24]'The disciple is not superior to his teacher, nor the slave to his master. [25]It is enough for the disciple that he should grow to be like his teacher, and the slave like his master. If they have called the master of the house Beelzebul, what will they not say of his household?

Open and fearless speech

[26]'Do not be afraid of them therefore. For everything that is now covered will be uncovered, and everything now hidden will be made clear. [27]What I say to you in the dark, tell in the daylight; what you hear in whispers, proclaim from the housetops.

[28]'Do not be afraid of those who kill the body but cannot kill the soul; fear him rather who can destroy both body and soul in hell. [29]Can you not buy two sparrows for a penny? And yet not one falls to the ground without your Father knowing. [30]Why, every hair on your head has been counted. [31]So there is no need to be afraid; you are worth more than hundreds of sparrows.

[32]'So if anyone declares himself for me in the presence of men, I will declare myself for him in the presence of

my Father in heaven. ³³But the one who disowns me in the presence of men, I will disown in the presence of my Father in heaven.

Jesus, the cause of dissension

³⁴"Do not suppose that I have come to bring peace to the earth: it is not peace I have come to bring, but a sword. ³⁵For I have come to set a man against his father, *a daughter against her mother, a daughter-in-law against her mother-in-law. ³⁶A man's enemies will be those of his own household.*[b]

Renouncing self to follow Jesus

³⁷"Anyone who prefers father or mother to me is not worthy of me. Anyone who prefers son or daughter to me is not worthy of me. ³⁸Anyone who does not take his cross and follow in my footsteps is not worthy of me. ³⁹Anyone who finds his life will lose it; anyone who loses his life for my sake will find it.

Conclusion

⁴⁰"Anyone who welcomes you welcomes me; and those who welcome me welcome the one who sent me.

⁴¹"Anyone who welcomes a prophet will have a prophet's reward; and anyone who welcomes a holy man will have a holy man's reward.

⁴²"If anyone gives so much as a cup of cold water to one of these little ones because he is a disciple, then I tell you solemnly, he will most certainly not lose his reward.'

---

10 b. Mt 7:6

IV. The Mystery of the Kingdom of Heaven

A. Narrative Section

11 [1]When Jesus had finished instructing his twelve disciples he moved on from there to teach and preach in their towns.[a]

The Baptist's question. Jesus commends him

[2]Now John in his prison had heard what Christ was doing and he sent his disciples to ask him, [3]'Are you the one who is to come, or have we got to wait for someone else?' [4]Jesus answered, 'Go back and tell John what you hear and see; [5]the blind see again, and the lame walk, lepers are cleansed, and the deaf hear, and the dead are raised to life and the Good News is proclaimed to the poor;[b] [6]and happy is the man who does not lose faith in me'.

[7]As the messengers were leaving, Jesus began to talk to the people about John: 'What did you go out into the wilderness to see? A reed swaying in the breeze? No? [8]Then what did you go out to see? A man wearing fine clothes? Oh no, those who wear fine clothes are to be found in palaces. [9]Then what did you go out for? To see a prophet? Yes, I tell you, and much more than a prophet: [10]he is the one of whom scripture says:

Look, I am going to send my messenger before you;

[11 a.] i.e. the Jews' towns.

[11 b.] These are signs of the messianic age in the prophecies of Isaiah.

he will prepare your way before you.[c]

[11]'I tell you solemnly, of all the children born of women, a greater than John the Baptist has never been seen; yet the least in the kingdom of heaven is greater than he is. [12]Since John the Baptist came, up to this present time, the kingdom of heaven has been subjected to violence and the violent are taking it by storm. [13]Because it was towards John that all the prophecies of the prophets and of the Law were leading; [14]and he, if you will believe me, is the Elijah who was to return.[d] [15]If anyone has ears to hear, let him listen!

Jesus condemns his contemporaries

[16]'What description can I find for this generation? It is like children shouting to each other as they sit in the market place:

[17]"We played the pipes for you,
and you wouldn't dance;
we sang dirges,
and you wouldn't be mourners".

[18]'For John came, neither eating nor drinking, and they say, "He is possessed". [19]The Son of Man came, eating and drinking, and they say, "Look, a glutton and a drunkard, a friend of tax collectors and sinners". Yet wisdom has been proved right by her actions.'

Lament over the lake-towns

[20]Then he began to reproach the towns in which most of his

[11c.] Ml 3:1

[11d.] According to the last of the prophets, Ml 3:23.

miracles had been worked, because they refused to repent.

[21]'Alas for you, Chorazin! Alas for you, Bethsaida! For if the miracles done in you had been done in Tyre and Sidon, they would have repented long ago in sackcloth and ashes. [22]And still, I tell you that it will not go as hard on Judgement day with Tyre and Sidon as with you. [23]And as for you, Capernaum, did you want to be exalted as high as heaven? *You shall be thrown down to hell.*[e] For if the miracles done in you had been done in Sodom, it would have been standing yet. [24]And still, I tell you that it will not go as hard with the land of Sodom on Judgement day as with you.'

The Good News revealed to the simple.
The Father and the Son
[25]At that time Jesus exclaimed, 'I bless you, Father, Lord of heaven and of earth, for hiding these things from the learned and the clever and revealing them to mere children. [26]Yes, Father, for that is what it pleased you to do. [27]Everything has been entrusted to me by my Father; and no one knows the Son except the Father, just as no one knows the Father except the Son and those to whom the Son chooses to reveal him.

The gentle mastery of Christ
[28]'Come to me, all you who labour and are overburdened, and I will give you rest. [29]Shoulder my yoke and learn from me, for I am gentle and humble in heart, *and you*

[11] e. Is 14

45

will find rest for your souls.[f] [30]Yes, my yoke is easy and my burden light.'

Picking corn on the sabbath

12[1]At that time Jesus took a walk one sabbath day through the cornfields. His disciples were hungry and began to pick ears of corn and eat them. [2]The Pharisees noticed it and said to him, 'Look, your disciples are doing something that is forbidden on the sabbath'. [3]But he said to them, 'Have you not read what David did when he and his followers were hungry - [4]how he went into the house of God and how they ate the loaves of offering which neither he nor his followers were allowed to eat, but which were for the priests alone? [5]Or again, have you not read in the Law that on the sabbath day the Temple priests break the sabbath without being blamed for it? [6]Now here, I tell you, is something greater than the Temple. [7]And if you had understood the meaning of the words: *What I want is mercy, not sacrifice*, you would not have condemned the blameless. [8]For the Son of Man is master of the sabbath.'

Cure of the man with a withered hand

[9]He moved on from there and went to their synagogue, [10]and a man was there at the time who had a withered hand. They asked him, 'Is it against the law to cure a man on the sabbath day?' hoping for something to use against him. [11]But he said to them, 'If any one of you here had only one sheep and it

[11f.] Jr 6:16

fell down a hole on the sabbath day, would he not get hold of it and lift it out? [12]Now a man is far more important than a sheep, so it follows that it is permitted to do good on the sabbath day.' [13]Then he said to the man, 'Stretch out your hand'. He stretched it out and his hand was better, as sound as the other one. [14]At this the Pharisees went out and began to plot against him, discussing how to destroy him.

Jesus the 'servant of Yahweh'

[15]Jesus knew this and withdrew from the district. Many followed him and he cured them all, [16]but warned them not to make him known. [17]This was to fulfil the prophecy of Isaiah:

[18]Here is my servant whom I have chosen,
my beloved, the favourite of my soul.
I will endow him with my spirit,
and he will proclaim the true faith to the nations.
[19]He will not brawl or shout,
nor will anyone hear his voice in the streets.
[20]He will not break the crushed reed,
nor put out the smouldering wick
till he has led the truth to victory:
[21]in his name the nations will put their hope.[a]

Jesus and Beelzebul

[22]Then they brought to him a blind and dumb demoniac; and he cured him, so that the dumb man could speak and see. [23]All the people were astounded and said, 'Can this

[12a.] Is 42:1-4.

be the Son of David?' [24]But when the Pharisees heard this they said, 'The man casts out devils only through Beelzebul,[b] the prince of devils'.

[25]Knowing what was in their minds he said to them, 'Every kingdom divided against itself is heading for ruin; and no town, no household divided against itself can stand. [26]Now if Satan casts out Satan, he is divided against himself; so how can his kingdom stand? [27]And if it is through Beelzebul that I cast out devils, through whom do your own experts cast them out? Let them be your judges, then. [28]But if it is through the Spirit of God that I cast devils out, then know that the kingdom of God has overtaken you.

[29]'Or again, how can anyone make his way into a strong man's house and burgle his property unless he has tied up the strong man first? Only then can he burgle his house.

[30]'He who is not with me is against me, and he who does not gather with me scatters. [31]And so I tell you, every one of men's sins and blasphemies will be forgiven, but blasphemy against the Spirit will not be forgiven. [32]And anyone who says a word against the Son of Man will be forgiven; but let anyone speak against the Holy Spirit and he will not be forgiven either in this world or in the next.

Words betray the heart
[33]'Make a tree sound and its fruit will be sound; make a

[12 b.] 'prince Baal' often contemptuously changed (e.g. 2 K 1:2f) to 'Beelzebub' 'Lord of the flies'.

tree rotten and its fruit will be rotten. For the tree can be told by its fruit. ³⁴Brood of vipers, how can your speech be good when you are evil? For a man's words flow out of what fills his heart. ³⁵A good man draws good things from his store of goodness; a bad man draws bad things from his store of badness. ³⁶So I tell you this, that for every unfounded word men utter they will answer on Judgement day, ³⁷since it is by your words you will be acquitted, and by your words condemned.'

The sign of Jonah

³⁸Then some of the scribes and Pharisees spoke up. 'Master,' they said 'we should like to see a sign^c from you.' ³⁹He replied, 'It is an evil and unfaithful generation that asks for a sign! The only sign it will be given is the sign of the prophet Jonah. ⁴⁰For as Jonah *was in the belly of the sea-monster for three days and three nights,^d* so will the Son of Man be in the heart of the earth for three days and three nights. ⁴¹On Judgement day the men of Nineveh will stand up with this generation and condemn it, because when Jonah preached they repented; and there is something greater than Jonah here. ⁴²On Judgement day the Queen of the South will rise up with this generation and condemn it, because she came from the ends of the earth to hear the wisdom of Solomon; and there is something greater than Solomon here.

---

¹² ᶜ A miracle to prove his authority.
¹² ᵈ Jon 2:1

The return of the unclean spirit

⁴³'When an unclean spirit goes out of a man it wanders through waterless country looking for a place to rest, and cannot find one. ⁴⁴Then it says, "I will return to the home I came from". But on arrival, finding it unoccupied, swept and tidied, ⁴⁵it then goes off and collects seven other spirits more evil than itself, and they go in and set up house there, so that the man ends up by being worse than he was before. That is what will happen to this evil generation.'

The true kinsmen of Jesus

⁴⁶He was still speaking to the crowds when his mother and his brothers° appeared; they were standing outside and were anxious to have a word with him. ⁴⁸But to the man who told him this Jesus replied, 'Who is my mother? Who are my brothers?' ⁴⁹And stretching out his hand towards his disciples he said, 'Here are my mother and my brothers. ⁵⁰Anyone who does the will of my Father in heaven, he is my brother and sister and mother.'

B. The Sermon of Parables

Introduction

13 ¹That same day, Jesus left the house and sat by the lakeside, ²but such large crowds gathered round him that he got into a boat and sat there. The people all stood

---

¹² ᵉ· In Hebr. and Aramaic (and many other languages), 'brothers' is the word used for cousins or even more distant relations of the same generation.

on the beach, [3]and he told them many things in parables.

Parable of the sower

He said, 'Imagine a sower going out to sow. [4]As he sowed, some seeds fell on the edge of the path, and the birds came and ate them up. [5]Others fell on patches of rock where they found little soil and sprang up straight away, because there was no depth of earth; [6]but as soon as the sun came up they were scorched and, not having any roots, they withered away. [7]Others fell among thorns, and the thorns grew up and choked them. [8]Others fell on rich soil and produced their crop, some a hundredfold, some sixty, some thirty. [9]Listen, anyone who has ears!'

Why Jesus speaks in parables

[10]Then the disciples went up to him and asked, 'Why do you talk to them in parables?' [11]'Because' he replied 'the mysteries of the kingdom of heaven are revealed to you, but they are not revealed to them. [12]For anyone who has will be given more, and he will have more than enough; but from anyone who has not, even what he has will be taken away. [13]The reason I talk to them in parables is that they look without seeing and listen without hearing or understanding. [14]So in their case this prophecy of Isaiah is being fulfilled:

You will listen and listen again, but not understand,
see and see again, but not perceive.
[15]*For the heart of this nation has grown coarse,*
their ears are dull of hearing, and they have shut their eyes,

for fear they should see with their eyes,
hear with their ears,
understand with their heart,
and be converted
and be healed by me.[a]

[16]'But happy are your eyes because they see, your ears because they hear! [17]I tell you solemnly, many prophets and holy men longed to see what you see, and never saw it; to hear what you hear, and never heard it.

The parable of the sower explained

[18]'You, therefore, are to hear the parable of the sower. [19]When anyone hears the word of the kingdom without understanding, the evil one comes and carries off what was sown in his heart: this is the man who received the seed on the edge of the path. [20]The one who received it on patches of rock is the man who hears the word and welcomes it at once with joy. [21]But he has no root in him, he does not last; let some trial come, or some persecution on account of the word, and he falls away at once. [22]The one who received the seed in thorns is the man who hears the word, but the worries of this world and the lure of riches choke the word and so he produces nothing. [23]And the one who received the seed in rich soil is the man who hears the word and understands it; he is the one who yields a harvest and produces now a hundredfold, now sixty, now thirty.'

[13a] Is 6:9-10

Parable of the darnel

[24]He put another parable before them, 'The kingdom of heaven may be compared to a man who sowed good seed in his field. [25]While everybody was asleep his enemy came, sowed darnel all among the wheat, and made off. [26]When the new wheat sprouted and ripened, the darnel appeared as well. [27]The owner's servants went to him and said, "Sir, was it not good seed that you sowed in your field? If so, where does the darnel come from?" [28]"Some enemy has done this" he answered. And the servants said, "Do you want us to go and weed it out?" [29]But he said, "No, because when you weed out the darnel you might pull up the wheat with it. [30]Let them both grow till the harvest; and at harvest time I shall say to the reapers: First collect the darnel and tie it in bundles to be burnt, then gather the wheat into my barn."'

Parable of the mustard seed

[31]He put another parable before them, 'The kingdom of heaven is like a mustard seed which a man took and sowed in his field. [32]It is the smallest of all the seeds, but when it has grown it is the biggest shrub of all and becomes a tree so that the birds of the air come and shelter in its branches.'

Parable of the yeast

[33]He told them another parable, 'The kingdom of heaven is like the yeast a woman took and mixed in with three measures of flour till it was leavened all through'.

The people are taught only in parables

[34]In all this Jesus spoke to the crowds in parables; indeed, he would never speak to them except in parables. [35]This was to fulfil the prophecy:

I will speak to you in parables
and expound things hidden since the foundation
of the world.[b]

The parable of the darnel explained

[36]Then, leaving the crowds, he went to the house; and his disciples came to him and said, 'Explain the parable about the darnel in the field to us'. [37]He said in reply, 'The sower of the good seed is the Son of Man. [38]The field is the world; the good seed is the subjects of the kingdom; the darnel, the subjects of the evil one; [39]the enemy who sowed them, the devil; the harvest is the end of the world; the reapers are the angels. [40]Well then, just as the darnel is gathered up and burnt in the fire, so it will be at the end of time. [41]The Son of Man will send his angels and they will gather out of his kingdom all things that provoke offences and all who do evil, [42]and throw them into the blazing furnace, where there will be weeping and grinding of teeth. [43]Then the virtuous will shine like the sun in the kingdom of their Father.[c] Listen, anyone who has ears!

13 b. Ps 78:2

13 c. The kingdom of the Son, v.41, is succeeded by the kingdom of the Father.

Parables of the treasure and of the pearl

[44]'The kingdom of heaven is like treasure hidden in a field which someone has found; he hides it again, goes off happy, sells everything he owns and buys the field.

[45]'Again, the kingdom of heaven is like a merchant looking for fine pearls; [46]when he finds one of great value he goes and sells everything he owns and buys it.

Parable of the dragnet

[47]'Again, the kingdom of heaven is like a dragnet cast into the sea that brings in a haul of all kinds. [48]When it is full, the fishermen haul it ashore; then, sitting down, they collect the good ones in a basket and throw away those that are no use. [49]This is how it will be at the end of time: the angels will appear and separate the wicked from the just [50]to throw them into the blazing furnace where there will be weeping and grinding of teeth.

Conclusion

[51]'Have you understood all this?' They said, 'Yes'. [52]And he said to them, 'Well then, every scribe who becomes a disciple of the kingdom of heaven is like a householder who brings out from his storeroom things both new and old'.[d]

[13 d.] Perhaps a saying of particular significance to Mt, a 'scribe who became a disciple'.

V. THE CHURCH, FIRST-FRUITS OF THE KINGDOM OF HEAVEN

A. Narrative Section

A visit to Nazareth

⁵³When Jesus had finished these parables he left the district; ⁵⁴and, coming to his home town,ᵉ he taught the people in their synagogue in such a way that they were astonished and said, 'Where did the man get this wisdom and these miraculous powers? ⁵⁵This is the carpenter's son, surely? Is not his mother the woman called Mary, and his brothers James and Joseph and Simon and Jude? ⁵⁶His sisters, too, are they not all here with us? So where did the man get it all?' ⁵⁷And they would not accept him. But Jesus said to them, 'A prophet is only despised in his own country and in his own house', ⁵⁸and he did not work many miracles there because of their lack of faith.

Herod and Jesus

14 ¹At that time Herod the tetrarch heard about the reputation of Jesus, ²and said to his court, 'This is John the Baptist himself; he has risen from the dead, and that is why miraculous powers are at work in him'.

John the Baptist beheaded

³Now it was Herod who had arrested John, chained him up and put him in prison because of Herodias, his brother

¹³ᵉ· Nazareth, see 2:23.

Philip's[a] wife. [4]For John had told him, 'It is against the Law for you to have her'. [5]He had wanted to kill him but was afraid of the people, who regarded John as a prophet. [6]Then, during the celebrations for Herod's birthday, the daughter of Herodias[b] danced before the company, and so delighted Herod [7]that he promised on oath to give her anything she asked. [8]Prompted by her mother she said, 'Give me John the Baptist's head, here, on a dish'. [9]The king was distressed but, thinking of the oaths he had sworn and of his guests, he ordered it to be given her, [10]and sent and had John beheaded in the prison. [11]The head was brought in on a dish and given to the girl who took it to her mother. [12]John's disciples came and took the body and buried it; then they went off to tell Jesus.

First miracle of the loaves

[13]When Jesus received this news he withdrew by boat to a lonely place where they could be by themselves. But the people heard of this and, leaving the towns, went after him on foot. [14]So as he stepped ashore he saw a large crowd; and he took pity on them and healed their sick.

[15]When evening came, the disciples went to him and said, 'This is a lonely place, and the time has slipped by; so send the people away, and they can go to the villages to buy themselves some food'. [16]Jesus replied, 'There is

---

[14a.] Philip, Herod's half-brother, was still alive.
[14b.] According to Josephus, the girl's name was Salome.

no need for them to go: give them something to eat yourselves'. [17]But they answered 'All we have with us is five loaves and two fish'. [18]'Bring them here to me' he said. [19]He gave orders that the people were to sit down on the grass; then he took the five loaves and the two fish, raised his eyes to heaven and said the blessing. And breaking the loaves handed them to his disciples who gave them to the crowds. [20]They all ate as much as they wanted, and they collected the scraps remaining; twelve baskets full. [21]Those who ate numbered about five thousand men, to say nothing of women and children.

Jesus walks on the water and, with him, Peter

[22]Directly after this he made the disciples get into the boat and go on ahead to the other side while he would send the crowds away. [23]After sending the crowds away he went up into the hills by himself to pray. When evening came, he was there alone, [24]while the boat, by now far out on the lake, was battling with a heavy sea, for there was a head-wind. [25]In the fourth watch of the night[c] he went towards them, walking on the lake, [26]and when the disciples saw him walking on the lake they were terrified. 'It is a ghost' they said, and cried out in fear. [27]But at once Jesus called out to them, saying, 'Courage! It is I! Do not be afraid.' [28]It was Peter who answered. 'Lord,' he said 'if it is you, tell me to come to you across the water.' [29]'Come' said Jesus. Then

---

[14][c] 3 to 6 a.m.

Peter got out of the boat and started walking towards Jesus across the water, ³⁰but as soon as he felt the force of the wind, he took fright and began to sink. 'Lord! Save me!' he cried. ³¹Jesus put out his hand at once and held him. 'Man of little faith,' he said 'why did you doubt?' ³²And as they got into the boat the wind dropped. ³³The men in the boat bowed down before him and said, 'Truly, you are the Son of God'.

Cures at Gennesaret

³⁴Having made the crossing, they came to land at Gennesaret. ³⁵When the local people recognised him they spread the news through the whole neighbourhood and took all that were sick to him, ³⁶begging him just to let them touch the fringe of his cloak. And all those who touched it were completely cured.

The traditions of the Pharisees

15 ¹Pharisees and scribes from Jerusalem then came to Jesus and said, ²'Why do your disciples break away from the tradition of the elders?ᵃ They do not wash their hands when they eat food.' ³'And why do you' he answered 'break away from the commandment of God for the sake of your tradition? ⁴For God said: *Do your duty toᵇ your father and mother and: Anyone who curses*

---

¹⁵ᵃ The traditional teaching, including many additions to and extensions of the Law.
¹⁵ᵇ Often translated 'honour', but the word implies a respect expressed in practical ways, Ex 20:12.

father or mother must be put to death.[c] [5]But you say, "If anyone says to his father or mother: Anything I have that I might have used to help you is dedicated to God", [6]he is rid of his duty to father or mother.[d] In this way you have made God's word null and void by means of your tradition. [7]Hypocrites! It was you Isaiah meant when he so rightly prophesied:

[8]*This people honours me only with lip-service,*
while their hearts are far from me.
[9]*The worship they offer me is worthless;*
the doctrines they teach are only human regulations.'[e]

On clean and unclean

[10]He called the people to him and said, 'Listen, and understand. [11]What goes into the mouth does not make a man unclean; it is what comes out of the mouth that makes him unclean.'

[12]Then the disciples came to him and said, 'Do you know that the Pharisees were shocked when they heard what you said?' [13]He replied, 'Any plant my heavenly Father has not planted will be pulled up by the roots. [14]Leave them alone. They are blind men leading blind men; and if one blind man leads another, both will fall into a pit.'

[15]At this, Peter said to him, 'Explain the parable for us'. [16]Jesus replied, 'Do even you not yet understand? [17]Can you

[15 c.] Lv 20:9
[15 d.] Property dedicated in this way could not be passed to another person.
[15 e.] Is 29:13

not see that whatever goes into the mouth passes through the stomach and is discharged into the sewer? [18]But the things that come out of the mouth come from the heart, and it is these that make a man unclean. [19]For from the heart come evil intentions: murder, adultery, fornication, theft, perjury, slander. [20]These are the things that make a man unclean. But to eat with unwashed hands does not make a man unclean.'

The daughter of the Canaanite woman healed

[21]Jesus left that place and withdrew to the region of Tyre and Sidon. [22]Then out came a Canaanite woman from that district and started shouting, 'Sir, Son of David, take pity on me. My daughter is tormented by a devil.' [23]But he answered her not a word. And his disciples went and pleaded with him. 'Give her what she wants,' they said 'because she is shouting after us.' [24]He said in reply, 'I was sent only to the lost sheep of the House of Israel'. [25]But the woman had come up and was kneeling at his feet. 'Lord,' she said 'help me.' [26]He replied, 'It is not fair to take the children's food and throw it to the house-dogs'. [27]She retorted, 'Ah yes, sir; but even house-dogs can eat the scraps that fall from their master's table'. [28]Then Jesus answered her, 'Woman, you have great faith. Let your wish be granted.' And from that moment her daughter was well again.

Cures near the lake

[29]Jesus went on from there and reached the shores of the Sea of Galilee, and he went up into the hills. He sat there,

³⁰and large crowds came to him bringing the lame, the crippled, the blind, the dumb and many others; these they put down at his feet, and he cured them. ³¹The crowds were astonished to see the dumb speaking, the cripples whole again, the lame walking and the blind with their sight, and they praised the God of Israel.

Second miracle of the loaves

³²But Jesus called his disciples to him and said, 'I feel sorry for all these people; they have been with me for three days now and have nothing to eat. I do not want to send them off hungry, they might collapse on the way.' ³³The disciples said to him, 'Where could we get enough bread in this deserted place to feed such a crowd?' ³⁴Jesus said to them, 'How many loaves have you?' 'Seven' they said 'and a few small fish.' ³⁵Then he instructed the crowd to sit down on the ground, ³⁶and he took the seven loaves and the fish, and he gave thanks and broke them and handed them to the disciples who gave them to the crowds. ³⁷They all ate as much as they wanted, and they collected what was left of the scraps, seven baskets full. ³⁸Now four thousand men had eaten, to say nothing of women and children. ³⁹And when he had sent the crowds away he got into the boat and went to the district of Magadan.

The Pharisees ask for a sign from heaven

16 ¹The Pharisees and Sadducees came, and to test him they asked if he would show them a sign from

heaven. [2]He replied, 'In the evening you say, "It will be fine; there is a red sky", [3]and in the morning, "Stormy weather today; the sky is red and overcast". You know how to read the face of the sky, but you cannot read the signs of the times. [4]It is an evil and unfaithful generation that asks for a sign! The only sign it will be given is the sign of Jonah.' And leaving them standing there, he went away.

The yeast of the Pharisees and Sadducees

[5]The disciples, having crossed to the other shore, had forgotten to take any food. [6]Jesus said to them, 'Keep your eyes open, and be on your guard against the yeast of the Pharisees and Sadducees'. [7]And they said to themselves, 'It is because we have not brought any bread'. [8]Jesus knew it, and he said, 'Men of little faith, why are you talking among yourselves about having no bread? [9]Do you not yet understand? Do you not remember the five loaves for the five thousand and the number of baskets you collected? [10]Or the seven loaves for the four thousand and the number of baskets you collected? [11]How could you fail to understand that I was not talking about bread? What I said was: Beware of the yeast of the Pharisees and Sadducees.' [12]Then they understood that he was telling them to be on their guard, not against the yeast for making bread, but against the teaching of the Pharisees and Sadducees.[a]

[16a] Yeast, here, is regarded as adulterating pure flour.

Peter's profession of faith; his pre-eminence

[13]When Jesus came to the region of Caesarea Philippi he put this question to his disciples, 'Who do people say the Son of Man is?' [14]And they said, 'Some say he is John the Baptist, some Elijah, and others Jeremiah or one of the prophets'. [15]'But you,' he said 'who do you say I am?' [16]Then Simon Peter spoke up, 'You are the Christ,' he said 'the Son of the living God'. [17]Jesus replied, 'Simon son of Jonah, you are a happy man! Because it was not flesh and blood that revealed this to you but my Father in heaven. [18]So I now say to you: You are Peter[b] and on this rock I will build my Church. And the gates of the underworld[c] can never hold out against it. [19]I will give you the keys of the kingdom of heaven: whatever you bind on earth shall be considered bound in heaven; whatever you loose on earth shall be considered loosed in heaven.'[d] [20]Then he gave the disciples strict orders not to tell anyone that he was the Christ.

First prophecy of the Passion

[21]From that time Jesus began to make it clear to his disciples that he was destined to go to Jerusalem and suffer grievously at the hands of the elders and chief priests and scribes, to be put to death and to be raised up on the third day. [22]Then, taking him aside, Peter started to remonstrate

---

[16 b.] Not, until now, a proper name: Greek petros (as in Engl. saltpetre) represents Aramaic kepha, rock.

[16 c.] The gates symbolise the power of the underworld to hold captives.

[16 d.] The keys have become the traditional insignia of Peter.

with him. 'Heaven preserve you, Lord;' he said 'this must not happen to you'. ²³But he turned and said to Peter, 'Get behind me, Satan! You are an obstacle in my path, because the way you think is not God's way but man's.'

The condition of following Christ

²⁴Then Jesus said to his disciples, 'If anyone wants to be a follower of mine, let him renounce himself and take up his cross and follow me. ²⁵For anyone who wants to save his life will lose it; but anyone who loses his life for my sake will find it. ²⁶What, then, will a man gain if he wins the whole world and ruins his life? Or what has a man to offer in exchange for his life?

²⁷'For the Son of Man is going to come in the glory of his Father with his angels, and, when he does, he will reward each one according to his behaviour. ²⁸I tell you solemnly, there are some of these standing here who will not taste death before they see the Son of Man coming with his kingdom.'ᵉ

The transfiguration

17 ¹Six days later, Jesus took with him Peter and James and his brother John and led them up a high mountain where they could be alone. ²There in their

---

¹⁶ᵉ. In vv. 27-28, two different sayings have been combined because both refer to the coming of the kingdom; but the first is about Judgement day, and the second is about the destruction of Jerusalem, the sign of 'the last days'.

presence he was transfigured: his face shone like the sun and his clothes became as white as the light. [3]Suddenly Moses and Elijah[a] appeared to them; they were talking with him. [4]Then Peter spoke to Jesus. 'Lord,' he said 'it is wonderful for us to be here; if you wish, I will make three tents here, one for you, one for Moses and one for Elijah.' [5]He was still speaking when suddenly a bright cloud covered them with shadow, and from the cloud there came a voice which said, 'This is my Son, the Beloved; he enjoys my favour. Listen to him.' [6]When they heard this the disciples fell on their faces overcome with fear. [7]But Jesus came up and touched them. 'Stand up,' he said 'do not be afraid.' [8]And when they raised their eyes they saw no one but only Jesus.

The question about Elijah

[9]As they came down from the mountain Jesus gave them this order, 'Tell no one about the vision until the Son of Man has risen from the dead'. [10]And the disciples put this question to him, 'Why do the scribes say then that Elijah has to come first?' [11]'True;' he replied 'Elijah is to come to see that everything is once more as it should be; [12]however, I tell you that Elijah has come already and they did not recognise him but treated him as they pleased; and the Son of Man will suffer similarly at their hands.' [13]The disciples understood then that he had been speaking of John the Baptist.

[17a] Representing the Law and the prophets.

The epileptic demoniac

[14]As they were rejoining the crowd a man came up to him and went down on his knees before him. [15]'Lord,' he said 'take pity on my son: he is a lunatic and in a wretched state; he is always falling into the fire or into the water. [16]I took him to your disciples and they were unable to cure him.' [17]'Faithless and perverse generation!' Jesus said in reply 'How much longer must I be with you? How much longer must I put up with you? Bring him here to me.' [18]And when Jesus rebuked it the devil came out of the boy who was cured from that moment.

[19]Then the disciples came privately to Jesus. 'Why were we unable to cast it out? they asked. [20]He answered, 'Because you have little faith. I tell you solemnly, if your faith were the size of a mustard seed you could say to this mountain, "Move from here to there", and it would move; nothing would be impossible for you.'

Second prophecy of the Passion

[22]One day when they were together in Galilee, Jesus said to them, 'The Son of Man is going to be handed over into the power of men; [23]they will put him to death, and on the third day he will be raised to life again'. And a great sadness came over them.

The Temple tax paid by Jesus and Peter

[24]When they reached Capernaum, the collectors of the half shekel[b] came to Peter and said, 'Does your master not pay

---

[17]b. A tax for the upkeep of the Temple.

the half-shekel?' ²⁵'Oh yes' he replied, and went into the house. But before he could speak, Jesus said, 'Simon, what is your opinion? From whom do the kings of the earth take toll or tribute? From their sons or from foreigners?' ²⁶And when he replied, 'From foreigners', Jesus said, 'Well then, the sons are exempt. ²⁷However, so as not to offend these people, go to the lake and cast a hook; take the first fish that bites, open its mouth and there you will find a shekel; take it and give it to them for me and for you.'

B. The Discourse on the Church

Who is the greatest?

18 ¹At this time the disciples came to Jesus and said, 'Who is the greatest in the kingdom of heaven?' ²So he called a little child to him and set the child in front of them. ³Then he said, 'I tell you solemnly, unless you change and become like little children you will never enter the kingdom of heaven. ⁴And so, the one who makes himself as little as this little child is the greatest in the kingdom of heaven.

On leading others astray

⁵'Anyone who welcomes a little child like this in my name welcomes me. ⁶But anyone who is an obstacle to bring down one of these little ones who have faith in me would be better drowned in the depths of the sea with a great millstone round his neck. ⁷Alas for the world that

there should be such obstacles! Obstacles indeed there must be, but alas for the man who provides them!

[8]'If your hand or your foot should cause you to sin, cut it off and throw it away: it is better for you to enter into life crippled or lame, than to have two hands or two feet and be thrown into eternal fire. [9]And if your eye should cause you to sin, tear it out and throw it away: it is better for you to enter into life with one eye, than to have two eyes and be thrown into the hell of fire.

[10]'See that you never despise any of these little ones, for I tell you that their angels in heaven are continually in the presence of my Father in heaven.[a]

The lost sheep

[12]'Tell me. Suppose a man has a hundred sheep and one of them strays; will he not leave the ninety-nine on the hillside and go in search of the stray? [13]I tell you solemnly, if he finds it, it gives him more joy than do the ninety-nine that did not stray at all. [14]Similarly, it is never the will of your Father in heaven that one of these little ones should be lost.

Brotherly correction

[15]'If your brother does something wrong, go and have it out with him alone, between your two selves. If he listens to you, you have won back your brother. [16]If he does not

---

[18 a.] V.11, at the time when verse numbers were added, consisted of a sentence which is not now accepted as part of the original text.

listen, take one or two others along with you: *the evidence of two or three witnesses is required to sustain any charge.* [17]But if he refuses to listen to these, report it to the community;[b] and if he refuses to listen to the community, treat him like a pagan or a tax collector.

[18]'I tell you solemnly, whatever you bind on earth shall be considered bound in heaven; whatever you loose on earth shall be considered loosed in heaven.

Prayer in common

[19]'I tell you solemnly once again, if two of you on earth agree to ask anything at all, it will be granted to you by my Father in heaven. [20]For where two or three meet in my name, I shall be there with them.'

Forgiveness of injuries

[21]Then Peter went up to him and said, 'Lord, how often must I forgive my brother if he wrongs me? As often as seven times?' [22]Jesus answered, 'Not seven, I tell you, but seventy-seven times.

Parable of the unforgiving debtor

[23]'And so the kingdom of heaven may be compared to a king who decided to settle his accounts with his servants. [24]When the reckoning began, they brought him a man who owed ten thousand talents;[c] [25]but he

---

[18 b.] The community of the brothers (the Church).
[18 c.] 'Millions of pounds' - about 20 years' wages for a labourer.

had no means of paying, so his master gave orders that he should be sold, together with his wife and children and all his possessions, to meet the debt. [26]At this, the servant threw himself down at his master's feet. "Give me time" he said "and I will pay the whole sum." [27]And the servant's master felt so sorry for him that he let him go and cancelled the debt. [28]Now as this servant went out, he happened to meet a fellow servant who owed him one hundred denarii;[d] and he seized him by the throat and began to throttle him. "Pay what you owe me" he said. [29]His fellow servant fell at his feet and implored him, saying, "Give me time and I will pay you". [30]But the other would not agree; on the contrary, he had him thrown into prison till he should pay the debt. [31]His fellow servants were deeply distressed when they saw what had happened, and they went to their master and reported the whole affair to him. [32]Then the master sent for him. "You wicked servant," he said "I cancelled all that debt of yours when you appealed to me. [33]Were you not bound, then, to have pity on your fellow servant just as I had pity on you?" [34]And in his anger the master handed him over to the torturers till he should pay all his debt. [35]And that is how my heavenly Father will deal with you unless you each forgive your brother from your heart.'

[18 d.] About 100 days' wages for a labourer.

VI. THE APPROACHING ADVENT OF THE KINGDOM OF HEAVEN

A. Narrative Section

The question about divorce

19 ¹Jesus had now finished what he wanted to say, and he left Galilee and came into the part of Judaea which is on the far side of the Jordan. ²Large crowds followed him and he healed them there.

³Some Pharisees approached him, and to test him they said, 'Is it against the Law for a man to divorce his wife on any pretext whatever?' ⁴He answered, 'Have you not read that the creator from the beginning *made them male and female* ⁵and that he said: *This is why a man must leave father and mother, and cling to his wife, and the two become one body?* ⁶They are no longer two, therefore, but one body. So then, what God has united, man must not divide'.

⁷They said to him, 'Then why did Moses command that a writ of dismissal should be given in cases of divorce?' ⁸'It was because you were so unteachable' he said 'that Moses allowed you to divorce your wives, but it was not like this from the beginning. ⁹Now I say this to you: the man who divorces his wife - I am not speaking of fornication - and marries another, is guilty of adultery.'

Continence

¹⁰The disciples said to him, 'If that is how things are between husband and wife, it is not advisable to marry'.

[11]But he replied, 'It is not everyone who can accept what I have said, but only those to whom it is granted. [12]There are eunuchs born that way from their mother's womb, there are eunuchs made so by men and there are eunuchs who have made themselves that way for the sake of the kingdom of heaven. Let anyone accept this who can.'

Jesus and the children

[13]People brought little children to him, for him to lay his hands on them and say a prayer. The disciples turned them away, [14]but Jesus said, 'Let the little children alone, and do not stop them coming to me; for it is to such as these that the kingdom of heaven belongs'. [15]Then he laid his hands on them and went on his way.

The rich young man

[16]And there was a man who came to him and asked, 'Master, what good deed must I do to possess eternal life?' [17]Jesus said to him, 'Why do you ask me about what is good? There is one alone who is good. But if you wish to enter into life, keep the commandments.' [18]He said, 'Which?' 'These:' Jesus replied *'You must not kill. You must not commit adultery. You must not bring false witness.* [19]*Honour your father and mother,* and: *you must love your neighbour as yourself.'*[a] [20]The young man said to him, 'I have kept all these. What more do I need to do?' [21]Jesus said, 'If you wish to be perfect, go and sell

[19 a.] Ex 20:12-16; Dt 5:16-20

what you own and give the money to the poor, and you will have treasure in heaven; then come, follow me'. [22]But when the young man heard these words he went away sad, for he was a man of great wealth.

The danger of riches

[23]Then Jesus said to his disciples, 'I tell you solemnly, it will be hard for a rich man to enter the kingdom of heaven. [24]Yes, I tell you again, it is easier for a camel to pass through the eye of a needle than for a rich man to enter the kingdom of heaven.' [25]When the disciples heard this they were astonished. 'Who can be saved, then?' they said. [26]Jesus gazed at them. 'For men' he told them 'this is impossible; for God everything is possible.'

The reward of renunciation

[27]Then Peter spoke. 'What about us?' he said to him 'We have left everything and followed you. What are we to have, then?' [28]Jesus said to him, 'I tell you solemnly, when all is made new and the Son of Man sits on his throne of glory, you will yourselves sit on twelve thrones to judge[b] the twelve tribes of Israel. [29]And everyone who has left houses, brothers, sisters, father, mother, children or land for the sake of my name will be repaid a hundred times over, and also inherit eternal life.

[30]'Many who are first will be last, and the last, first.

[19 b.] i.e. to govern.

Parable of the vineyard labourers

20 ¹'Now the kingdom of heaven is like a landowner going out at daybreak to hire workers for his vineyard. ²He made an agreement with the workers for one denarius a day, and sent them to his vineyard. ³Going out at about the third hour he saw others standing idle in the market place ⁴and said to them, "You go to my vineyard too and I will give you a fair wage". ⁵So they went. At about the sixth hour and again at about the ninth hour, he went out and did the same. ⁶Then at about the eleventh hour he went out and found more men standing round, and he said to them, "Why have you been standing here idle all day?" ⁷"Because no one has hired us" they answered. He said to them, "You go into my vineyard too". ⁸In the evening, the owner of the vineyard said to his bailiff, "Call the workers and pay them their wages, starting with the last arrivals and ending with the first". ⁹So those who were hired at about the eleventh hour came forward and received one denarius each. ¹⁰When the first came, they expected to get more, but they too received one denarius each. ¹¹They took it, but grumbled at the landowner. ¹²"The men who came last" they said "have done only one hour, and you have treated them the same as us, though we have done a heavy day's work in all the heat." ¹³He answered one of them and said, "My friend, I am not being unjust to you; did we not agree on one denarius? ¹⁴Take your earnings and go. I choose to pay the last comer as much as I pay you. ¹⁵Have I no right to

do what I like with my own? Why be envious because I am generous?" [16]Thus the last will be first, and the first, last.'

Third prophecy of the Passion

[17]Jesus was going up to Jerusalem, and on the way he took the Twelve to one side and said to them, [18]'Now we are going up to Jerusalem, and the Son of Man is about to be handed over to the chief priests and scribes. They will condemn him to death [19]and will hand him over to the pagans to be mocked and scourged and crucified; and on the third day he will rise again.'

The mother of Zebedee's sons makes her request

[20]Then the mother of Zebedee's sons came with her sons to make a request of him, and bowed low; [21]and he said to her, 'What is it you want?' She said to him, 'Promise that these two sons of mine may sit one at your right hand and the other at your left in your kingdom'. [22]'You do not know what you are asking' Jesus answered. 'Can you drink the cup that I am going to drink?' They replied, 'We can'. [23]'Very well,' he said 'you shall drink my cup[a], but as for seats at my right hand and my left, these are not mine to grant; they belong to those to whom they have been allotted by my Father.'

Leadership with service

[24]When the other ten heard this they were indignant with

---

[20][a]. Perhaps a prophecy of the martyrdom of James and John; James was certainly put to death by Herod Agrippa about 44 A.D., Ac 12:2.

the two brothers. ²⁵But Jesus called them to him and said, 'You know that among the pagans the rulers lord it over them, and their great men make their authority felt. ²⁶This is not to happen among you. No; anyone who wants to be great among you must be your servant, ²⁷and anyone who wants to be first among you must be your slave, ²⁸just as the Son of Man came not to be served but to serve, and to give his life as a ransom for many.'

The two blind men of Jericho

²⁹As they left Jericho a large crowd followed him. ³⁰Now there were two blind men sitting at the side of the road. When they heard that it was Jesus who was passing by, they shouted, 'Lord! Have pity on us, Son of David.' ³¹And the crowd scolded them and told them to keep quiet, but they only shouted more loudly, 'Lord! Have pity on us, Son of David.' ³²Jesus stopped, called them over and said, 'What do you want me to do for you?' ³³They said to him, 'Lord, let us have our sight back'. ³⁴Jesus felt pity for them and touched their eyes, and immediately their sight returned and they followed him.

The Messiah enters Jerusalem

21 ¹When they were near Jerusalem and had come in sight of Bethphage on the Mount of Olives, Jesus sent two disciples, ²saying to them, 'Go to the village facing you, and you will immediately find a tethered donkey and a colt with her. Untie them and bring them to

me. ³If anyone says anything to you, you are to say, "The Master needs them and will send them back directly".' ⁴This took place to fulfil the prophecy:

> ⁵*Say to the daughter of Zion:*
> *Look, your king comes to you;*
> *he is humble, he rides on a donkey*
> *and on a colt, the foal of a beast of burden.ᵃ*

⁶So the disciples went out and did as Jesus had told them. ⁷They brought the donkey and the colt, then they laid their cloaks on their backs and he sat on them. ⁸Great crowds of people spread their cloaks on the road, while others were cutting branches from the trees and spreading them in his path. ⁹The crowds who went in front of him and those who followed were all shouting:

> '*Hosanna*ᵇ to the Son of David!
> *Blessings on who comes in the name of the Lord!*ᶜ
> *Hosanna* in the highest heavens!'

¹⁰And when he entered Jerusalem, the whole city was in turmoil. 'Who is this?' people asked, ¹¹and the crowds answered, 'This is the prophet Jesus from Nazareth in Galilee'.

The expulsion of the dealers from the Temple
¹²Jesus then went into the Temple and drove out all those who were selling and buying there; he upset the tables of

---

²¹ᵃ· Is 62:11; Zc 9:9
²¹ᵇ· Conventional shout of acclaim, like a cheer.
²¹ᶜ· Ps 118:26

the money changers and the chairs of those who were selling pigeons.[d] [13]'According to scripture' he said *'my house will be called a house of prayer[e]*; but you are turning it into a *robbers' den[f]*. [14]There were also blind and lame people who came to him in the Temple, and he cured them. [15]At the sight of the wonderful things he did and of the children shouting, 'Hosanna to the Son of David' in the Temple, the chief priests and the scribes were indignant. [16]'Do you hear what they are saying?' they said to him. 'Yes,' Jesus answered 'have you never read this:

By the mouths of children, babes in arms,
you have made sure of praise?'[g]

[17]With that he left them and went out of the city to Bethany where he spent the night.

The barren fig tree withers. Faith and prayer

[18]As he was returning to the city in the early morning, he felt hungry. [19]Seeing a fig tree by the road, he went up to it and found nothing on it but leaves. And he said to it, 'May you never bear fruit again'; and at that instant the fig tree withered. [20]The disciples were amazed when they saw it. 'What happened to the tree' they said 'that it withered there and then?' [21]Jesus answered, 'I tell you

---

[21d.] Money changers provided Temple currency, and the traders the animals, for making sacrificial offerings.
[21e.] Is 56:7
[21f.] Jr 7:11
[21g.] Ps 8:2 (LXX); Ws 10:21

solemnly, if you have faith and do not doubt at all, not only will you do what I have done to the fig tree, but even if you say to this mountain, "Get up and throw yourself into the sea", it will be done. [22]And if you have faith, everything you ask for in prayer you will receive.'

The authority of Jesus is questioned

[23]He had gone into the Temple and was teaching, when the chief priests and the elders of the people came to him and said, 'What authority have you for acting like this? And who gave you this authority?' [24]'And I' replied Jesus 'will ask you a question, only one; if you tell me the answer to it, I will then tell you my authority for acting like this. [25]John's baptism: where did it come from: heaven or man?' And they argued it out this way among themselves, 'If we say from heaven, he will retort, "Then why did you refuse to believe him?"; [26]but if we say from man, we have the people to fear, for they all hold that John was a prophet'. [27]So their reply to Jesus was, 'We do not know'. And he retorted, 'Nor will I tell you my authority for acting like this.

Parable of the two sons

[28]'What is your opinion? A man had two sons. He went and said to the first, "My boy, you go and work in the vineyard today". [29]He answered, "I will not go", but afterwards thought better of it and went. [30]The man then went and said the same thing to the second who answered, "Certainly, sir", but did not go. [31]Which of the

two did the father's will?' 'The first' they said. Jesus said to them, 'I tell you solemnly, tax collectors and prostitutes are making their way into the kingdom of God before you. ³²For John came to you, a pattern of true righteousness, but you did not believe him, and yet the tax collectors and prostitutes did. Even after seeing that, you refused to think better of it and believe in him.

Parable of the wicked husbandmen

³³'Listen to another parable. There was a man, a landowner, who planted a vineyard; he fenced it round, dug a winepress in it and built a tower; then he leased it to tenants and went abroad. ³⁴When vintage time drew near he sent his servants to the tenants to collect his produce. ³⁵But the tenants seized his servants, thrashed one, killed another and stoned a third. ³⁶Next he sent some more servants, this time a larger number, and they dealt with them in the same way. ³⁷Finally he sent his son to them. "They will respect my son" he said. ³⁸But when the tenants saw the son, they said to each other, "This is the heir. Come on, let us kill him and take over his inheritance." ³⁹So they seized him and threw him out of the vineyard and killed him. ⁴⁰Now when the owner of the vineyard comes, what will he do to those tenants?' ⁴¹They answered, 'He will bring those wretches to a wretched end and lease the vineyard to other tenants who will deliver the produce to him when the season arrives'. ⁴²Jesus said to them, 'Have you never read in the scriptures:

> *It was the stone rejected by the builders*
> *that became the keystone.*
> *This was the Lord's doing*
> *and it is wonderful to see?*[h]

[43]I tell you, then, that the kingdom of God will be taken from you and given to a people who will produce its fruit.'

[45]When they heard his parables, the chief priests and the scribes realised he was speaking about them, [46]but though they would have liked to arrest him they were afraid of the crowds, who looked on him as a prophet.

Parable of the wedding feast

22 [1]Jesus began to speak to them in parables once again, [2]'The kingdom of heaven may be compared to a king who gave a feast for his son's wedding. [3]He sent his servants to call those who had been invited, but they would not come. [4]Next he sent some more servants. "Tell those who have been invited" he said "that I have my banquet all prepared, my oxen and fattened cattle have been slaughtered, everything is ready. Come to the wedding." [5]But they were not interested: one went off to his farm, another to his business, [6]and the rest seized his servants, maltreated them and killed them. [7]The king was furious. He despatched his troops, destroyed those murderers and burnt their town. [8]Then he said to his servants, "The wedding is ready; but as those who were invited proved to be unworthy, [9]go to the crossroads in the town and invite

---

[21][h] Ps 118:22-23

everyone you can find to the wedding". [10]So these servants went out on to the roads and collected together everyone they could find, bad and good alike; and the wedding hall was filled with guests. [11]When the king came in to look at the guests he noticed one man who was not wearing a wedding garment, [12]and said to him, "How did you get in here, my friend, without a wedding garment?" And the man was silent. [13]Then the king said to the attendants, "Bind him hand and foot and throw him out into the dark, where there will be weeping and grinding of teeth". [14]For many are called, but few are chosen.'

On tribute to Caesar

[15]Then the Pharisees went away to work out between them how to trap him in what he said. [16]And they sent their disciples to him, together with the Herodians,[a] to say, 'Master, we know that you are an honest man and teach the way of God in an honest way, and that you are not afraid of anyone, because a man's rank means nothing to you. [17]Tell us your opinion, then. Is it permissible to pay taxes to Caesar or not?' [18]But Jesus was aware of their malice and replied, 'You hypocrites! Why do you set this trap for me? [19]Let me see the money you pay the tax with.' They handed him a denarius, [20]and he said, 'Whose head is this? Whose name?' [21]'Caesar's'

---

[22][a] Supporters of the ruling family, hoping to find a cause for denouncing Jesus to the Romans.

they replied. He then said to them, 'Very well, give back to Caesar what belongs to Caesar - and to God what belongs to God'. ²²This reply took them by surprise, and they left him alone and went away.

The resurrection of the dead

²³That day some Sadducees - who deny that there is a resurrection - approached him and they put this question to him, ²⁴'Master, Moses said that if a man dies childless, his brother is to marry the widow, his sister-in-law to raise children for his brother. ²⁵Now we had a case involving seven brothers; the first married and then died without children, leaving his wife to his brother; ²⁶the same thing happened with the second and third and so on to the seventh, ²⁷and then last of all the woman herself died. ²⁸Now at the resurrection to which of those seven will she be wife, since she had been married to them all?' ²⁹Jesus answered them, 'You are wrong, because you understand neither the scriptures nor the power of God. ³⁰For at the resurrection men and women do not marry; no, they are like the angels in heaven. ³¹And as for the resurrection of the dead, have you never read what God himself said to you: ³²*I am the God of Abraham, the God of Isaac and the God of Jacob?*ᵇ God is God, not of the dead, but of the living.' ³³And his teaching made a deep impression on the people who heard it.

---

²² b. Ex 3:6

The greatest commandment of all

³⁴But when the Pharisees heard that he had silenced the Sadducees they got together ³⁵and, to disconcert him, one of them put a question, ³⁶'Master, which is the greatest commandment of the Law?' ³⁷Jesus said, '*You must love the Lord your God with all your heart, with all your soul,* and with all your mind. ³⁸This is the greatest and the first commandment. ³⁹The second resembles it: *You must love your neighbour as yourself.* ⁴⁰On these two commandments hang the whole Law, and the Prophets also.'

Christ not only son but also Lord of David

⁴¹While the Pharisees were gathered round, Jesus put to them this question, ⁴²'What is your opinion about the Christ? Whose son is he?' 'David's' they told him. ⁴³'Then how is it' he said 'that David, moved by the Spirit, calls him Lord, where he says:

⁴⁴*The Lord said to my Lord:*
Sit at my right hand
and I will put your enemies
under your feet?^c

⁴⁵'If David can call him Lord, then how can he be his son?' ⁴⁶Not one could think of anything to say in reply, and from that day no one dared to ask him any further questions.

---

^{22 c.} Ps 110:1

The scribes and Pharisees: their hypocrisy and vanity

23 [1]Then addressing the people and his disciples Jesus said, [2]'The scribes and the Pharisees occupy the chair of Moses. [3]You must therefore do what they tell you and listen to what they say; but do not be guided by what they do: since they do not practise what they preach. [4]They tie up heavy burdens and lay them on men's shoulders, but will they lift a finger to move them? Not they! [5]Everything they do is done to attract attention, like wearing broader phylacteries and longer tassels[a], [6]like wanting to take the place of honour at banquets and the front seats in the synagogues, [7]being greeted obsequiously in the market squares and having people call them Rabbi.

[8]'You, however, must not allow yourselves to be called Rabbi, since you have only one master, and you are all brothers. [9]You must call no one on earth your father, since you have only one Father, and he is in heaven. [10]Nor must you allow yourselves to be called teachers, for you have only one Teacher, the Christ. [11]The greatest among you must be your servant. [12]Anyone who exalts himself will be humbled, and anyone who humbles himself will be exalted.

The sevenfold indictment of the scribes and Pharisees

[13]'Alas for you, scribes and Pharisees, you hypocrites! You who shut up the kingdom of heaven in men's faces, neither

---

[23 a.] Phylacteries: containers for short texts taken from the Law; they were worn on the arm or the forehead in obedience to Ex 13:9,16 and Dt 6:8. The tassels were sewn to the corners of the cloak.

going in yourselves nor allowing others to go in[b] who want to.

[15]'Alas for you, scribes and Pharisees, you hypocrites! You who travel over sea and land to make a single proselyte, and when you have him you make him twice as fit for hell as you are.

[16]'Alas for you, blind guides! You who say, "If a man swears by the Temple, it has no force; but if a man swears by the gold of the Temple, he is bound". [17]Fools and blind! For which is of greater worth, the gold or the Temple that makes the gold sacred? [18]Or else, "If a man swears by the altar it has no force; but if a man swears by the offering that is on the altar, he is bound". [19]You blind men! For which is of greater worth, the offering or the altar that makes the offering sacred? [20]Therefore, when a man swears by the altar he is swearing by that and by everything on it. [21]And when a man swears by the Temple he is swearing by that and by the One who dwells in it. [22]And when a man swears by heaven he is swearing by the throne of God and by the One who is seated there.

[23]'Alas for you, scribes and Pharisees, you hypocrites! You who pay your tithe of mint and dill and cummin[c] and have neglected the weightier matters of the Law - justice, mercy, good faith! These you should have practised, without neglecting the others. [24]You blind guides! Straining out gnats and swallowing camels!

[23 b.] By interpreting the Law so strictly that nobody could obey all of it.
[23 c.] The law of paying tithes on crops was extended to include herbs and plants grown for flavouring.

[25]'Alas for you, scribes and Pharisees, you hypocrites! You who clean the outside of cup and dish and leave the inside full of extortion and intemperance. [26]Blind Pharisee! Clean the inside of cup and dish first so that the outside may become clean as well.

[27]'Alas for you, scribes and Pharisees, you hypocrites! You who are like whitewashed tombs that look handsome on the outside, but inside are full of dead men's bones and every kind of corruption. [28]In the same way you appear to people from the outside like good honest men, but inside you are full of hypocrisy and lawlessness.

[29]'Alas for you, scribes and Pharisees, you hypocrites! You who build the sepulchres of the prophets and decorate the tombs of holy men, [30]saying, "We would never have joined in shedding the blood of the prophets, had we lived in our fathers' day". [31]So! Your own evidence tells against you! You are the sons of those who murdered the prophets! [32]Very well then, finish off the work that your fathers began.

Their crimes and approaching punishment

[33]'Serpents, brood of vipers, how can you escape being condemned to hell? [34]This is why, in my turn, I am sending you prophets and wise men and scribes: some you will slaughter and crucify, some you will scourge in your synagogues and hunt from town to town; [35]and so you will draw down on yourselves the blood of every holy man that has been shed on earth, from the blood of

Abel the Holy to the blood of Zechariah son of Barachiah[d] whom you murdered between the sanctuary and the altar. [36]I tell you solemnly, all of this will recoil on this generation.

Jerusalem admonished

[37]'Jerusalem, Jerusalem, you that kill the prophets and stone those who are sent to you! How often have I longed to gather your children, as a hen gathers her chicks under her wings, and you refused! [38]So be it! Your house will be left to you desolate, [39]for, I promise, you shall not see me any more until you say:

Blessings on him who comes in the name of the Lord!'[e]

B. The Sermon on the End

Introduction

24[1]Jesus left the Temple, and as he was going away his disciples came up to draw his attention to the Temple buildings. [2]He said to them in reply, 'You see all these? I tell you solemnly, not a single stone here will be left on another: everything will be destroyed.' [3]And when he was sitting on the Mount of Olives the disciples came and asked him privately, 'Tell us, when is this going to happen, and what will be the sign of your coming and of the end of the world?'

[23 d.] Possibly Zechariah, the last of the prophets to be killed, according to the Jewish scriptures (2 Ch 24:20-22).
[23 e.] Ps 118:26

The beginning of sorrows

⁴And Jesus answered them, 'Take care that no one deceives you; ⁵because many will come using my name and saying, "I am the Christ", and they will deceive many. ⁶You will hear of wars and rumours of wars; do not be alarmed, for this is something that must happen, but the end will not be yet. ⁷For nation will fight against nation, and kingdom against kingdom. There will be famines and earthquakes here and there. ⁸All this is only the beginning of the birthpangs.

⁹'Then they will hand you over to be tortured and put to death; and you will be hated by all the nations on account of my name. ¹⁰And then many will fall away; men will betray one another and hate one another. ¹¹Many false prophets will arise; they will deceive many, ¹²and with the increase of lawlessness, love in most men will grow cold; ¹³but the man who stands firm to the end will be saved.

¹⁴'This Good News of the kingdom will be proclaimed to the whole worldᵃ as a witness to all the nations. And then the endᵇ will come.

The great tribulation of Jerusalem

¹⁵'So when you see *the disastrous abomination*, of which the prophet Daniel spoke, set up in the Holy Place (let the reader understand), ¹⁶then those in Judaea must escape to the mountains; ¹⁷if a man is on the housetop, he must not

---

²⁴ᵃ· The 'inhabited world' as it was known.
²⁴ᵇ· The fall and destruction of Jerusalem. A prophecy of this is combined, in this discourse, with descriptions of the 'last days'.

come down to collect his belongings; [18]if a man is in the fields, he must not turn back to fetch his cloak. [19]Alas for those with child, or with babies at the breast, when those days come! [20]Pray that you will not have to escape in winter or on a sabbath. [21]For then there will be *great distress such as, until now, since* the world began, there never *has been*, nor ever will be again. [22]And if that time had not been shortened, no one would have survived; but shortened that time shall be, for the sake of those who are chosen.

[23]'If anyone says to you then, "Look, here is the Christ" or, "He is there", do not believe it; [24]for false Christs and false prophets will arise and produce great signs and portents, enough to deceive even the chosen, if that were possible. [25]There; I have forewarned you.

The coming of the Son of Man will be evident
[26]'If, then, they say to you, "Look, he is in the desert", do not go there; "Look, he is in some hiding place", do not believe it; [27]because the coming of the Son of Man will be like lightning striking in the east and flashing far into the west. [28]Wherever the corpse is, there will the vultures gather.

The universal significance of this coming
[29]'Immediately after the distress of those days[c] the sun will be darkened, the moon will lose its brightness, the stars will fall from the sky and the powers of heaven will be shaken. [30]And then the sign of the Son of Man will appear in

---

[24 c.] Join with v.22. vv. 23-28 are a digression.

heaven; then too all the peoples of the earth will beat their breasts; and they will see the Son of Man coming on the clouds of heaven with power and great glory.[d] [31]And he will send his angels with a loud trumpet to gather his chosen from the four winds, from one end of heaven to the other.

The time of this coming

[32]'Take the fig tree as a parable: as soon as its twigs grow supple and its leaves come out, you know that summer is near. [33]So with you when you see all these things: know that he is near, at the very gates. [34]I tell you solemnly, before this generation has passed away all these things will have taken place.[e] [35]Heaven and earth will pass away, but my words will never pass away. [36]But as for that day and hour, nobody knows it, neither the angels of heaven, nor the Son, no one but the Father only.

Be on the alert

[37]'As it was in Noah's day, so will it be when the Son of Man comes. [38]For in those days before the Flood people were eating, drinking, taking wives, taking husbands, right up to the day Noah went into the ark, [39]and they suspected nothing till the Flood came and swept all away. It will be like this when the Son of Man comes. [40]Then of two men in the fields one is taken, one left; [41]of two women at the millstone grinding, one is taken, one left.

[24 d.] As foretold in Dn 7:14.
[24 e.] Meaning the fall and destruction of Jerusalem.

⁴²'So stay awake, because you do not know the day when your master is coming. ⁴³You may be quite sure of this that if the householder had known at what time of the night the burglar would come, he would have stayed awake and would not have allowed anyone to break through the wall of his house. ⁴⁴Therefore, you too must stand ready because the Son of Man is coming at an hour you do not expect.

Parable of the conscientious steward

⁴⁵'What sort of servant, then, is faithful and wise enough for the master to place him over his household to give them their food at the proper time? ⁴⁶Happy that servant if his master's arrival finds him at this employment. ⁴⁷I tell you solemnly, he will place him over everything he owns. ⁴⁸But as for the dishonest servant who says to himself, "My master is taking his time", ⁴⁹and sets about beating his fellow servants and eating and drinking with drunkards, ⁵⁰his master will come on a day he does not expect and at an hour he does not know. ⁵¹The master will cut him off and send him to the same fate as the hypocrites, where there will be weeping and grinding of teeth.

Parable of the ten bridesmaids

25 ¹'Then the kingdom of heaven will be like this: Ten bridesmaids took their lamps and went to meet the bridegroom. ²Five of them were foolish and five were sensible: ³the foolish ones did take their lamps, but they brought no oil, ⁴whereas the sensible ones took

flasks of oil as well as their lamps. [5]The bridegroom was late, and they all grew drowsy and fell asleep. [6]But at midnight there was a cry, "The bridegroom is here! Go out and meet him." [7]At this, all those bridesmaids woke up and trimmed their lamps, [8]and the foolish ones said to the sensible ones, "Give us some of your oil: our lamps are going out". [9]But they replied, "There may not be enough for us and for you; you had better go to those who sell it and buy some for yourselves". [10]They had gone off to buy it when the bridegroom arrived. Those who were ready went in with him to the wedding hall and the door was closed. [11]The other bridesmaids arrived later. "Lord, Lord," they said "open the door for us." [12]But he replied, "I tell you solemnly, I do not know you". [13]So stay awake, because you do not know either the day or the hour.

Parable of the talents

[14]"It is like a man on his way abroad who summoned his servants and entrusted his property to them. [15]To one he gave five talents, to another two, to a third one; each in proportion to his ability. Then he set out. [16]The man who had received the five talents promptly went and traded with them and made five more. [17]The man who had received two made two more in the same way. [18]But the man who had received one went off and dug a hole in the ground and hid his master's money. [19]Now a long time after, the master of those servants came back and went through his accounts with them. [20]The man who had received the five talents came

forward bringing five more. "Sir," he said "you entrusted me with five talents; here are five more that I have made." [21]His master said to him, "Well done, good and faithful servant; you have shown you can be faithful in small things, I will trust you with greater; come and join in your master's happiness". [22]Next the man with the two talents came forward. "Sir," he said "you entrusted me with two talents; here are two more that I have made." [23]His master said to him, "Well done, good and faithful servant; you have shown you can be faithful in small things, I will trust you with greater; come and join in your master's happiness". [24]Last came forward the man who had the one talent. "Sir," said he "I had heard you were a hard man, reaping where you have not sown and gathering where you have not scattered; [25]so I was afraid, and I went off and hid your talent in the ground. Here it is; it was yours, you have it back." [26]But his master answered him, "You wicked and lazy servant! So you knew that I reap where I have not sown and gather where I have not scattered? [27]Well then, you should have deposited my money with the bankers, and on my return I would have recovered my capital with interest. [28]So now, take the talent from him and give it to the man who has the five talents. [29]For to everyone who has will be given more, and he will have more than enough; but from the man who has not, even what he has will be taken away. [30]As for this good-for-nothing servant, throw him out into the dark, where there will be weeping and grinding of teeth."

The Last Judgement

[31]'When the Son of Man comes in his glory, escorted by all the angels, then he will take his seat on his throne of glory. [32]All the nations will be assembled before him and he will separate men one from another as the shepherd separates sheep from goats. [33]He will place the sheep on his right hand and the goats on his left. [34]Then the King will say to those on his right hand, "Come, you whom my Father has blessed, take for your heritage the kingdom prepared for you since the foundation of the world. [35]For I was hungry and you gave me food; I was thirsty and you gave me drink; I was a stranger and you made me welcome; [36]naked and you clothed me, sick and you visited me, in prison and you came to see me." [37]Then the virtuous will say to him in reply, "Lord, when did we see you hungry and feed you; or thirsty and give you drink? [38]When did we see you a stranger and make you welcome; naked and clothe you; [39]sick or in prison and go to see you?" [40]And the King will answer, "I tell you solemnly, in so far as you did this to one of the least of these brothers of mine, you did it to me". [41]Next he will say to those on his left hand, "Go away from me, with your curse upon you, to the eternal fire prepared for the devil and his angels. [42]For I was hungry and you never gave me food; I was thirsty and you never gave me anything to drink; [43]I was a stranger and you never made me welcome, naked and you never clothed me, sick and in prison and you never visited me." [44]Then it will be their turn

to ask, "Lord, when did we see you hungry or thirsty, a stranger or naked, sick or in prison, and did not come to your help?" [45]Then he will answer, "I tell you solemnly, in so far as you neglected to do this to one of the least of these, you neglected to do it to me". [46]And they will go away to eternal punishment, and the virtuous to eternal life.'

VII. PASSION AND RESURRECTION

The conspiracy against Jesus

26 [1]Jesus had now finished all he wanted to say, and he told his disciples, [2]'It will be Passover, as you know, in two days' time, and the Son of Man will be handed over to be crucified'.

[3]Then the chief priests and the elders of the people assembled in the palace of the high priest, whose name was Caiaphas, [4]and made plans to arrest Jesus by some trick and have him put to death. [5]They said, however, 'It must not be during the festivities; there must be no disturbance among the people'.

The anointing at Bethany

[6]Jesus was at Bethany in the house of Simon the leper, when [7]a woman came to him with an alabaster jar of the most expensive ointment, and poured it on his head as he was at table. [8]When they saw this, the disciples were indignant; 'Why this waste?' they said. [9]'This could have been sold at a high price and the money given to the poor.' [10]Jesus noticed

this. 'Why are you upsetting the woman?' he said to them. 'What she has done for me is one of the good works[a] indeed! [11]You have the poor with you always, but you will not always have me. [12]When she poured this ointment on my body, she did it to prepare me for burial. [13]I tell you solemnly, wherever in all the world this Good News is proclaimed, what she has done will be told also, in remembrance of her.'

Judas betrays Jesus

[14]Then one of the Twelve, the man called Judas Iscariot, went to the chief priests and said, [15]'What are you prepared to give me if I hand him over to you?' [16]They paid him thirty silver pieces[b], and from that moment he looked for an opportunity to betray him.

Preparations for the Passover supper

[17]Now on the first day of Unleavened Bread[c] the disciples came to Jesus to say, 'Where do you want us to make the preparations for you to eat the passover?' [18]'Go to so-and-so in the city' he replied 'and say to him, "The Master says: My time is near. It is at your house that I am keeping Passover with my disciples."' [19]The disciples did what Jesus told them and prepared the Passover.

[26 a.] As 'good works', charitable deeds were reckoned superior to almsgiving.

[26 b.] 30 shekels, the price fixed for a slave's life, Ex 21:32.

[26 c.] Unleavened bread was normally to be eaten during the seven days which followed the Passover supper; here the writer appears to mean the first day of the whole Passover celebration.

The treachery of Judas foretold

[20]When evening came he was at table with the twelve disciples. [21]And while they were eating he said 'I tell you solemnly, one of you is about to betray me'. [22]They were greatly distressed and started asking him in turn, 'Not I, Lord, surely?' [23]He answered, 'Someone who has dipped his hand into the dish with me, will betray me. [24]The Son of Man is going to his fate, as the scriptures say he will, but alas for that man by whom the Son of Man is betrayed! Better for that man if he had never been born!' [25]Judas, who was to betray him; asked in his turn, 'Not I, Rabbi, surely?' 'They are your own words' answered Jesus.

The institution of the Eucharist

[26]Now as they were eating[d], Jesus took some bread, and when he had said the blessing he broke it and gave it to the disciples. 'Take it and eat;' he said 'this is my body.' [27]Then he took a cup, and when he had returned thanks he gave it to them. 'Drink all of you from this,' he said [28]'for this is my blood, the blood of the covenant, which is to be poured out for many for the forgiveness of sins. [29]From now on, I tell you, I shall not drink wine until the day I drink the new wine with you in the kingdom of my Father.'

---

[26][d.] The Passover supper itself, for which exact rules for the blessing of bread and wine were laid down. The 'eating' of v.21 is the first course, which came before the Passover itself.

Peter's denial foretold

³⁰After psalms had been sung[e] they left for the Mount of Olives. ³¹Then Jesus said to them, 'You will all lose faith in me this night,[f] for the scripture says: *I shall strike the shepherd and the sheep of the flock will be scattered,*[g] ³²but after my resurrection I shall go before you to Galilee'. ³³At this, Peter said, 'Though all lose faith in you, I will never lose faith'. ³⁴Jesus answered him, 'I tell you solemnly, this very night, before the cock crows, you will have disowned me three times'. ³⁵Peter said to him, 'Even if I have to die with you, I will never disown you'. And all the disciples said the same.

Gethsemane

³⁶Then Jesus came with them to a small estate called Gethsemane; and he said to his disciples, 'Stay here while I go over there to pray'. ³⁷He took Peter and the two sons of Zebedee with him. And sadness came over him, and great distress. ³⁸Then he said to them, 'My soul is sorrowful to the point of death. Wait here and keep awake with me.' ³⁹And going on a little further he fell on his face and prayed. 'My Father,' he said 'if it is possible, let this cup pass me by. Nevertheless, let it be as you, not I, would have it.' ⁴⁰He came back to the disciples and found them sleeping, and he

---

²⁶ ᵉ. The psalms of praise which end the Passover supper.

²⁶ ᶠ. 'be brought down': the regular expression for the losing of faith through a difficulty or blow to it.

²⁶ ᵍ. Zc 13:7

said to Peter, 'So you had not the strength to keep awake with me one hour? [41]You should be awake, and praying not to be put to the test. The spirit is willing, but the flesh is weak.' [42]Again, a second time, he went away and prayed: 'My Father,' he said 'If this cup cannot pass by without my drinking it, your will be done!' [43]And he came back again and found them sleeping, their eyes were so heavy. [44]Leaving them there, he went away again and prayed for the third time, repeating the same words. [45]Then he came back to the disciples and said to them, 'You can sleep on now and take your rest. Now the hour has come when the Son of Man is to be betrayed into the hands of sinners. [46]Get up! Let us go! My betrayer is already close at hand.'

The arrest

[47]He was still speaking when Judas, one of the Twelve, appeared, and with him a large number of men armed with swords and clubs, sent by the chief priests and elders of the people. [48]Now the traitor had arranged a sign with them. 'The one I kiss,' he had said 'he is the man. Take him in charge.' [49]So he went straight up to Jesus and said, 'Greetings, Rabbi', and kissed him. [50]Jesus said to him, 'My friend, do what you are here for'. Then they came forward, seized Jesus and took him in charge. [51]At that, one of the followers of Jesus grasped his sword and drew it; he struck out at the high priest's servant, and cut off his ear. [52]Jesus then said, 'Put your sword back, for all who draw the sword will die by the sword. [53]Or do you think that I

cannot appeal to my Father who would promptly send more than twelve legions of angels to my defence? [54]But then, how would the scriptures be fulfilled that say this is the way it must be?' [55]It was at this time that Jesus said to the crowds, 'Am I a brigand, that you had to set out to capture me with swords and clubs? I sat teaching in the Temple day after day and you never laid hands on me.' [56]Now all this happened to fulfil the prophecies in scripture. Then all the disciples deserted him and ran away.

Jesus before the Sanhedrin

[57]The men who had arrested Jesus led him off to Caiaphas the high priest, where the scribes and the elders were assembled. [58]Peter followed him at a distance, and when he reached the high priest's palace, he went in and sat down with the attendants to see what the end would be.

[59]The chief priests and the whole Sanhedrin were looking for evidence against Jesus, however false, on which they might pass the death-sentence. [60]But they could not find any, though several lying witnesses came forward. Eventually two stepped forward [61]and made a statement, 'This man said, "I have power to destroy the Temple of God and in three days build it up"' [62]The high priest then stood up and said to him, 'Have you no answer to that? What is this evidence these men are bringing against you?' [63]But Jesus was silent. And the high priest said to him, 'I put you on oath by the living God to tell us if you are the Christ, the Son of God'.

⁶⁴'The words are your own' answered Jesus. 'Moreover, I tell you that from this time onward you will see the *Son of Man seated at the right hand of the Power and coming on the clouds of heaven*.' ⁶⁵At this, the high priest tore his clothes and said, 'He has blasphemed. What need of witnesses have we now? There! You have just heard the blasphemy. ⁶⁶What is your opinion?' They answered, 'He deserves to die'.

⁶⁷Then they spat in his face and hit him with their fists; others said as they struck him, ⁶⁸'Play the prophet, Christ! Who hit you then?'

Peter's denials

⁶⁹Meanwhile Peter was sitting outside in the courtyard, and a servant-girl came up to him and said, 'You too were with Jesus the Galilean'. ⁷⁰But he denied it in front of them all. 'I do not know what you are talking about' he said. ⁷¹When he went out to the gateway another servant-girl saw him and said to the people there, 'This man was with Jesus the Nazarene'. ⁷²And again, with an oath, he denied it, 'I do not know the man'. ⁷³A little later the bystanders came up and said to Peter, 'You are one of them for sure! Why, your accent gives you away.' ⁷⁴Then he started calling down curses on himself and swearing, 'I do not know the man'. At that moment the cock crew, ⁷⁵and Peter remembered what Jesus had said, 'Before the cock crows you will have disowned me three times'. And he went outside and wept bitterly.

Jesus is taken before Pilate

27 ¹When morning came, all the chief priests and the elders of the people met in council to bring about the death of Jesus. ²They had him bound, and led him away to hand him over to Pilate[a], the governor.

The death of Judas

³When he found that Jesus had been condemned, Judas his betrayer was filled with remorse and took the thirty silver pieces back to the chief priests and elders. ⁴'I have sinned;' he said 'I have betrayed innocent blood'. 'What is that to us?' they replied 'That is your concern.' ⁵And flinging down the silver pieces in the sanctuary he made off and hanged himself; ⁶The chief priests picked up the silver pieces and said, 'It is against the Law to put this into the treasury; it is blood-money'. ⁷So they discussed the matter and bought the potter's field with it as a graveyard for foreigners, ⁸and this is why the field is called the Field of Blood today. ⁹The words of the prophet Jeremiah[b] were then fulfilled: *And they took the thirty silver pieces, the sum at which the precious One was priced by children of Israel, ¹⁰and they gave them for the potter's field, just as the Lord directed me.*

Jesus before Pilate

¹¹Jesus, then, was brought before the governor, and the

---

[a] The Jews had to approach the Roman governor for confirmation and execution of any sentence of death.
[b] Actually a free quotation from Zc 11:12-13.

governor put to him this question, 'Are you the king of the Jews?' Jesus replied, 'It is you who say it'. [12]But when he was accused by the chief priests and the elders he refused to answer at all. [13]Pilate then said to him, 'Do you not hear how many charges they have brought against you?' [14]But to the governor's complete amazement, he offered no reply to any of the charges.

[15]At festival time it was the governor's practice to release a prisoner for the people, anyone they chose. [16]Now there was at that time a notorious prisoner whose name was Barabbas. [17]So when the crowd gathered, Pilate said to them, 'Which do you want me to release for you: Barabbas, or Jesus who is called Christ?' [18]For Pilate knew it was out of jealousy that they had handed him over.

[19]Now as he was seated in the chair of judgement, his wife sent him a message, 'Have nothing to do with that man; I have been upset all day by a dream I had about him'.

[20]The chief priests and the elders, however, had persuaded the crowd to demand the release of Barabbas and the execution of Jesus. [21]So when the governor spoke and asked them, 'Which of the two do you want me to release for you?' they said, 'Barabbas'. [22]'But in that case,' Pilate said to them 'what am I to do with Jesus who is called Christ?' They all said, 'Let him be crucified!' [23]'Why?' he asked 'What harm has he done?' But they shouted all the louder, 'Let him be crucified!' [24]Then Pilate saw that he was making no impression, that

in fact a riot was imminent. So he took some water, washed his hands in front of the crowd and said, 'I am innocent of this man's blood. It is your concern.' ²⁵And the people, to a man, shouted back, 'His blood be on us and on our children!' ²⁶Then he released Barabbas for them. He ordered Jesus to be first scourged[c] and then handed over to be crucified.

Jesus is crowned with thorns

²⁷The governor's soldiers took Jesus with them into the Praetorium and collected the whole cohort round him. ²⁸Then they stripped him and made him wear a scarlet cloak, ²⁹and having twisted some thorns into a crown they put this on his head and placed a reed in his right hand. To make fun of him they knelt to him saying, 'Hail, king of the Jews!' ³⁰And they spat on him and took the reed and struck him on the head with it. ³¹And when they had finished making fun of him, they took off the cloak and dressed him in his own clothes and led him away to crucify him.

The crucifixion

³²On their way out, they came across a man from Cyrene, Simon by name, and enlisted him to carry his cross. ³³When they had reached a place called Golgotha[d], that is,

---

²⁷ᶜ The normal prelude to crucifixion.
²⁷ᵈ The Aramaic form of the name of which Calvary is the more familiar Latin equivalent.

the place of the skull, [34]they gave him wine to drink mixed with gall, which he tasted but refused to drink. [35]When they had finished crucifying him they shared out his clothing by casting lots, [36]and then sat down nd stayed there keeping guard over him.

[37]Above his head was placed the charge against him it read: 'This is Jesus, the King of the Jews'. [38]At the sar time two robbers were crucified with him, one on tl right and one on the left.

The crucified Christ is mocked

[39]The passers-by jeered at him; they shook their heads [40]and said, 'So you would destroy the Temple and rebuild it in three days! Then save yourself! If you are God's son, come down from the cross!' [41]The chief priests with the scribes and elders mocked him in the same way. [42]'He saved others;' they said 'he cannot save himself. He is the king of Israel; let him come down from the cross now, and we will believe in him. [43]He puts his trust in God; now let God rescue him if he wants him. For he did say, "I am the son of God".' [44]Even the robbers who were crucified with him taunted him in the same way.

The death of Jesus

[45]From the sixth hour there was darkness over all the land until the ninth hour[e]. [46]And about the ninth hour, Jesus cried out in a loud voice, 'Eli, Eli, lama sabachthani?' that

---

[27 e.] From mid-day to 3 p.m.

is, *'My God, my God, why have you deserted me?'* [f] [47]When some of those who stood there heard this, they said, 'The man is calling on Elijah', [48]and one of them quickly ran to get a sponge which he dipped in vinegar[g] and, putting it on a reed, gave it him to drink. [49]'Wait!' said the rest of them 'and see if Elijah will come to save him.' [50]But Jesus, again crying out in a loud voice, yielded up his spirit.

[51]At that, the veil of the Temple[h] was torn in two from top to bottom; the earth quaked; the rocks were split; [52]the tombs opened and the bodies of many holy men rose from the dead, [53]and these, after his resurrection, came out of the tombs, entered the Holy City and appeared to a number of people. [54]Meanwhile the centurion, together with the others guarding Jesus, had seen the earthquake and all that was taking place, and they were terrified and said, 'In truth this was a son of God.'

[55]And many women were there, watching from a distance, the same women who had followed Jesus from Galilee and looked after him. [56]Among them were Mary of Magdala, Mary the mother of James and Joseph, and the mother of Zebedee's sons.

The burial

[57]When it was evening, there came a rich man of Arimathaea, called Joseph, who had himself become a

---

27 f. Ps 22:1

27 g. The rough wine drunk by Roman soldiers.

27 h. There were two curtains in the Temple; most probably this was the inner curtain which guarded the Most Holy Place.

disciple of Jesus. [58]This man went to Pilate and asked for the body of Jesus. Pilate thereupon ordered it to be handed over. [59]So Joseph took the body, wrapped it in a clean shroud [60]and put it in his own new tomb which he had hewn out of the rock. He then rolled a large stone across the entrance of the tomb and went away. [61]Now Mary of Magdala and the other Mary were there, sitting opposite the sepulchre.

The guard at the tomb

[62]Next day, that is, when Preparation Day[i] was over, the chief priests and the Pharisees went in a body to Pilate [63]and said to him, 'Your Excellency, we recall that this impostor said, while he was still alive, "After three days I shall rise again". [64]Therefore give the order to have the sepulchre kept secure until the third day, for fear his disciples come and steal him away and tell the people, "He has risen from the dead". This last piece of fraud would be worse than what went before.' [65]'You may have your guard' said Pilate to them. 'Go and make all as secure as you know how.' [66]So they went and made the sepulchre secure, putting seals on the stone and mounting a guard.

The empty tomb. The angel's message

28 [1]After the sabbath, and towards dawn on the first day of the week, Mary of Magdala and the other Mary went to visit the sepulchre. [2]And all at once there was a violent earthquake, for the angel of the Lord,

---

[27 i.] The day before the sabbath.

descending from heaven, came and rolled away the stone and sat on it. ³His face was like lightning, his robe white as snow. ⁴The guards were so shaken, so frightened of him, that they were like dead men. ⁵But the angel spoke; and he said to the women, 'There is no need for you to be afraid. I know you are looking for Jesus, who was crucified. ⁶He is not here, for he has risen, as he said he would. Come and see the place where he lay, ⁷then go quickly and tell his disciples, "He has risen from the dead and now he is going before you to Galilee; it is there you will see him". Now I have told you.' ⁸Filled with awe and great joy the women came quickly away from the tomb and ran to tell the disciples.

Appearance to the women

⁹And there, coming to meet them, was Jesus. 'Greetings' he said. And the women came up to him and, falling down before him, clasped his feet. ¹⁰Then Jesus said to them, 'Do not be afraid; go and tell my brothers that they must leave for Galilee; they will see me there'.

Precautions taken by the leaders of the people

¹¹While they were on their way, some of the guard went off into the city to tell the chief priests all that had happened. ¹²These held a meeting with the elders and, after some discussion, handed a considerable sum of money to the soldiers ¹³with these instructions, 'This is what you must say, "His disciples came during the night and stole him away

while we were asleep". ¹⁴And should the governor come to hear of this, we undertake to put things right with him ourselves and to see that you do not get into trouble.' ¹⁵The soldiers took the money and carried out their instructions, and to this day that is the story among the Jews.

Appearance in Galilee. The mission to the world

¹⁶Meanwhile the eleven disciples set out for Galilee, to the mountain where Jesus had arranged to meet them. ¹⁷When they saw him they fell down before him, though some hesitated. ¹⁸Jesus came up and spoke to them. He said, 'All authority in heaven and on earth has been given to me. ¹⁹Go, therefore, make disciples of all the nations; baptise them in the name of the Father and of the Son and of the Holy Spirit,[a] ²⁰and teach them to observe all the commands I gave you. And know that I am with you always; yes, to the end of time.'

[28 a.] This formula is perhaps a reflection of the liturgical usage of the writer's own time.